First World War
and Army of Occupation
War Diary
France, Belgium and Germany

17 DIVISION
51 Infantry Brigade,
Brigade Machine Gun Company
14 February 1916 - 28 February 1918

WO95/2008/3

The Naval & Military Press Ltd
www.nmarchive.com
Published in association with The National Archives

Published by

The Naval & Military Press Ltd

Unit 10 Ridgewood Industrial Park,

Uckfield, East Sussex,

TN22 5QE England

Tel: +44 (0) 1825 749494

www.naval-military-press.com

www.nmarchive.com

This diary has been reprinted in facsimile from the original. Any imperfections are inevitably reproduced and the quality may fall short of modern type and cartographic standards.

© **Crown Copyright**
Images reproduced by permission of The National Archives, London, England, 2015.

Contents

Document type	Place/Title	Date From	Date To
Heading	2008/3 51 Infantry Brigade Brigade Machine Gun Corps 1916 Feb-1918 Feb		
Heading	17th Division 51st Infy Bde 51st Machine Gun Coy. Feb 1916-Feb 1918		
War Diary	Bluff	14/02/1916	02/03/1916
War Diary	Reninghelst	05/03/1916	06/03/1916
War Diary	Armentieres	18/03/1916	19/03/1916
War Diary	Bluff S. of Ypres	02/03/1916	02/03/1916
War Diary	Reninghelst	06/03/1916	16/03/1916
War Diary	Armentieres	18/03/1916	17/05/1916
War Diary	Armentieres	07/05/1916	07/05/1916
War Diary	Armentieres	04/05/1916	04/05/1916
War Diary	Petit Difques	18/05/1916	31/05/1916
Heading	51st Bde Machine Gun Coy D.A.G. G.H.Q. 3 Echelon Herewith War Diary for June Please ask receipt here on.		
War Diary	St Omer	01/06/1916	12/06/1916
War Diary	Allonville	12/06/1916	12/06/1916
War Diary	Heilly	27/06/1916	27/06/1916
War Diary	Morlancourt	30/06/1916	30/06/1916
Heading	51st Inf. Bde. 17th Div. War Diary 51st Machine Gun Company. July 1916		
War Diary	Morlancourt	01/07/1916	01/07/1916
War Diary	Fricourt	03/07/1916	04/07/1916
War Diary	Ville	06/07/1916	06/07/1916
War Diary	Fricourt	06/07/1916	06/07/1916
War Diary	Meaulte	11/07/1916	11/07/1916
War Diary	Fordrinov	12/07/1916	12/07/1916
War Diary	Bussus	14/07/1916	14/07/1916
War Diary	Buire	23/07/1916	23/07/1916
Heading	51st Brigade. 17th Division. 51st Brigade Machine Gun Company August 1916		
Heading	War Diary 51st Machine Gun Company. August 1916 Vol 7		
War Diary	Buire	01/08/1916	01/08/1916
War Diary	Mametz	04/08/1916	12/08/1916
War Diary	Buire	15/08/1916	15/08/1916
War Diary	Gezaincourt	15/08/1916	15/08/1916
War Diary	Bienvillers	20/08/1916	31/08/1916
War Diary	Hannescamp	01/09/1916	11/09/1916
War Diary	Halloy	12/09/1916	12/09/1916
War Diary	Bayencourt	15/09/1916	15/09/1916
War Diary	Hebuterne	16/09/1916	20/09/1916
War Diary	Humber Camp	20/09/1916	20/09/1916
War Diary	Doullens	22/09/1916	22/09/1916
War Diary	Outrebois	23/09/1916	23/09/1916
War Diary	Maison-Ponthieu	24/09/1916	30/09/1916
Heading	War Diary 51st Machine Gun Company Oct 1916 Vol 9		
War Diary	Maison Ponthieu	28/09/1916	28/09/1916
War Diary	Left Maison Ponthieu	01/10/1916	01/10/1916
War Diary	Frohon Le Petit	02/10/1916	02/10/1916

War Diary	Halloy	03/10/1916	03/10/1916
War Diary	Bayencourt	04/10/1916	04/10/1916
War Diary	Hebuterne	05/10/1916	05/10/1916
War Diary	Souastre	14/10/1916	14/10/1916
War Diary	Lucheux	19/10/1916	19/10/1916
War Diary	Treux	22/10/1916	22/10/1916
War Diary	Citadel F 21 b	27/10/1916	27/10/1916
War Diary	Le Transloy Line N. 28+34	31/10/1916	31/10/1916
Heading	War Diary of 51st Machine Gun Coy. For November 1916 Volume I		
War Diary	N. 28 Sheet 57c 1/20,000	01/11/1916	01/11/1916
War Diary	N. 28.a. 8.9 to N. 28.C. 4.5	03/11/1916	03/11/1916
War Diary	From N. 28 Sheet 57c to A. 8.a.8.2	08/11/1916	08/11/1916
War Diary	C. Camp S. 23.b. 5.3	12/11/1916	13/11/1916
War Diary	H. Camp To Meaulte	13/11/1916	13/11/1916
War Diary	C. Camp To Mansel Camp	14/11/1916	14/11/1916
War Diary	Mansel Camp To Meaulte	15/11/1916	15/11/1916
War Diary	Meaulte To Divisional Rest area.	15/11/1916	15/11/1916
War Diary	Meaulte To Soues	16/11/1916	16/11/1916
War Diary	Soues	17/11/1916	11/12/1916
War Diary	Soues To Corbie	12/12/1916	12/12/1916
War Diary	Corbie	13/12/1916	22/12/1916
War Diary	Corbie To Meaulte	23/12/1916	23/12/1916
War Diary	Meaulte To Camp 22 Carnoy East	24/12/1916	24/12/1916
War Diary	Camp 22 Carnoy E. To Mansel Camp F. 11.b.	26/12/1916	26/12/1916
War Diary	Mansel Camp To Camps 18 & 21 Carnoy E.	30/12/1916	30/12/1916
War Diary	Camps 18+21 Carnoy E. To Guillemont Ref. S Coy 57	31/12/1916	31/12/1916
War Diary	Mansel Camp To Camps 18-21 Carnoy E. And Goillemont	31/12/1916	31/12/1916
War Diary	Lesboeufs Sector Map reference of Coy F/9-S.24 B.9.4	01/01/1917	15/01/1917
War Diary	S.24.b. 9.4 To Camp 21 Carnoy East	15/01/1917	15/01/1917
War Diary	Camp 21 Carnoy To Meaulte	16/01/1917	16/01/1917
War Diary	Meaulte	17/01/1917	23/01/1917
War Diary	Meaulte To Bronfay Farm	24/01/1917	24/01/1917
War Diary	Bronfay Farm To Maltz Horn	25/01/1917	25/01/1917
War Diary	Maltz Horn To T. 23.b. 5.3	27/01/1917	27/01/1917
War Diary	T. 23.b. 5.3	28/01/1917	31/01/1917
War Diary	In The Line Coy Y Q at T. 23.b. 53.	01/02/1917	13/02/1917
War Diary	T. 23.b 53 to Bronfay Farm	14/02/1917	16/02/1917
War Diary	Bronfay Farm	17/02/1917	18/02/1917
War Diary	Bronfay To Flesselles	19/02/1917	19/02/1917
War Diary	Bronfay To Franvillers	20/02/1917	20/02/1917
War Diary	Franvillers To Bussy Les Daours	21/02/1917	21/02/1917
War Diary	Bussy	22/02/1917	25/02/1917
Heading	War Diary Volume I of 51st Machine Gun Company for March 1917 Vol 14		
War Diary	Bussy Les Daours	01/03/1917	01/03/1917
War Diary	Rubempre	02/03/1917	12/03/1917
War Diary	Longuevillette	13/03/1917	13/03/1917
War Diary	Neuilly Le Dien	14/03/1917	14/03/1917
War Diary	Cherienne	15/03/1917	21/03/1917
War Diary	Mamur Farm (Buire Au Bois)	22/03/1917	22/03/1917
War Diary	Brevillers	23/03/1917	23/03/1917
War Diary	Oppy	24/03/1917	30/06/1917
War Diary	Beaudricourt To Y. Huts.	01/05/1917	31/05/1917
War Diary	Pommera To Saulty	01/06/1917	09/06/1917

War Diary	Pommera To St Nicholas Camps	22/06/1917	22/06/1917
War Diary	St. Nicholas Camps Into Line.	29/06/1917	29/06/1917
War Diary	In Line	30/06/1917	30/06/1917
War Diary	Company Headquarter Map Reference Biache 1/20,000 H 5 D 8.0	01/07/1917	14/07/1917
War Diary	Company Headquarter Map Reference Biache 1/20,000 H 17 C 2.6	14/07/1917	31/07/1917
War Diary	In The Field	01/08/1917	09/12/1917
War Diary	Field	09/12/1917	20/12/1917
War Diary	In The Field	20/12/1917	31/12/1917
Heading	7th (Westmorland And Cumberland Yeomanry) Bn. Border Regt War Diary For January 1918 Vol 30		
War Diary	In The Field	01/01/1918	01/02/1918
Miscellaneous	51st Inf. Bde	01/03/1918	01/03/1918
War Diary	In The Field	01/02/1918	08/02/1918
War Diary	Field	08/02/1918	23/02/1918
War Diary	Salamanca & Vittoria Camps	24/02/1918	28/02/1918

2008/3

51 Infantry Brigade

Brigade Machine Gun Company.

1916 Feb – 1916 Feb

17TH DIVISION
51ST INFY BDE

51ST MACHINE GUN COY.
FEB 1916 - FEB 1918

Army Form C. 2118

WAR DIARY
or
INTELLIGENCE SUMMARY
(Erase heading not required.)

51st Brigade Machine Gun Coy

Place	Date	Hour	Summary of Events and Information	Remarks and references to Appendices
BLUFF	14/2/16	11 PM	During the German attack on the BLUFF on 14 & 16 the Company was ordered to support the defence. Eight guns were placed in the line and 4 kept in reserve. The guns had to take up their positions under a very heavy enemy artillery fire but did not suffer any loss. The Brigade was withdrawn on the 15th July but the Company remained in with the relieving Brigade (76th).	
"	2/3/16	4:30 am	During the attack the Company was attached to the Brigade detailed to recapture lost trenches. Ten guns were employed for this & six kept in reserve. The attack was very successful and the casualties in the Company, notwithstanding the furious bombardment, were two gunners. They were subject for 28 hours to a furious bombardment.	
			The Company was relieved on the 12th March to go into rest. It was praised during these operations first, owing to its firmness of its personnel, secondly because was then too arduous a task for more	
			The company of machine guns — best troops were sent as Tuesday to set from	

Army Form C. 2118

WAR DIARY
or
INTELLIGENCE SUMMARY
(Erase heading not required.)

51/st Machine Gun Cy. Vol A.

Place	Date	Hour	Summary of Events and Information	Remarks and references to Appendices
BLUFF	March 1st	–	The Company was attached to the 76th Brigade for the recapture of the trenches lost at the BLUFF on the YPRES-COMINES Canal on Feb. 14th	
"	2nd	4.30am	The trenches were retaken on the morning of Feb 2nd at 4.30 a.m. 8 Vickers guns were in position to repel counter attacks & kept in reserve. One gun only had an opportunity to come into action & fired about 2000 rounds. This gun team had 2 men wounded, viz. O/o JACKAMAN and HATLEY, the former carrying no other casualties though subject to an intense bombardment for 28 hours.	
RENINGHE-LST	5	10 PM	The company returned to BILLETS.	
"	6	12.30PM	Marched to STEENWERK for 12 days rest in Billets. during this period training was carried on.	
ARMENTIÈ-RES	18	11 am	Arrived and went into Billets in ARMENTIÈRES. Billets very good.	
"	19	10 am	8 guns sent into the line at LA CHAPELLE D'ARMENTIÈRES; 4 guns in strong posts & 4 in subsidiary line. The existing emplacements required very considerable improvement & a good deal of work was carried out. The positions for night firing had been very badly chosen, being only a few yards from	
"	–	–		

Army Form C. 2118

WAR DIARY of the 51st Bde. Machine Gun Coy.
or
INTELLIGENCE SUMMARY

(Erase heading not required.)

SIMGCoy
Vol 2.

17th

Instructions regarding War Diaries and Intelligence Summaries are contained in F. S. Regs., Part II. and the Staff Manual respectively. Title Pages will be prepared in manuscript.

Place	Date	Hour	Summary of Events and Information	Remarks and references to Appendices
BLUFF S. of YPRES.	Mch 2nd 1916	-	The Company was attached to the 76th Brigade, 3rd Div. for the recapture of the trenches lost at the BLUFF on the 14th February 1916. 8 guns were placed; three in the front line and five in redoubts in rear of support line. Two guns kept in reserve at (Bde. H. Qrs. the remaining 6 guns were with the 51st Bde, who were reserve to the 76th. One gun in the front line fired during the Bombardment & covered the advance of a portion of the attacking infantry. The other guns had special orders to deal with Counter attacks. The operations were entirely successful. There were only two Casualties in the Coy.; 2 men wounded.	
RENINGHELST	Mch 6/16	12.15 P.m.	The Company marched to rest Billets.	
ARMENTIERES.	Mch 18/16	-	Arrived at ARMENTIERES.	
"	Mch 19.		Took over the line from the 63rd Bde. M.G.C. near LA CHAPELLE d'ARMENTIERES. Eight guns in the line & 8 resting in Billets; the Coy. relieving itself by half Coys every 8 days. The eight guns were at first disposed in the Strong Points & the Subsidiary line.	

WAR DIARY or INTELLIGENCE SUMMARY

51st M.G.C.

Army Form C. 2118

Place	Date	Hour	Summary of Events and Information	Remarks and references to Appendices
ARMENTIERES	heh		The battle emplacements constructed. Fresh positions were chosen & further emplacements constructed. Indirect fire with two guns commenced & continued nightly.	
	25	6.30 Pm		
	26	11 am	Receipt of 8 guns by the 8 in rest carried out. There is nothing of special importance to report during the month of March beyond the action at the BLUFF. It was found that owing to casualties from sickness, due to snowy weather, it was very difficult to keep the gun teams at full strength. The establishment being only 4 men per gun. This also entailed trouble journeys in getting guns, ammunition re men per gun. At the end of the month 32 men from the Infy Bns were attached for a course of 3 weeks instruction with a view of keeping the guns fully manned & also to enable 12 guns to be relieved in the line.	

Ogilvy Capt

Army Form C. 2118

WAR DIARY 51st Machine Gun Coy

or

INTELLIGENCE SUMMARY

(Erase heading not required.)

Instructions regarding War Diaries and Intelligence Summaries are contained in F.S. Regs., Part II. and the Staff Manual respectively. Title Pages will be prepared in manuscript.

Place	Date	Hour	Summary of Events and Information	Remarks and references to Appendices
ARMENTIERES	1.4.16.	—	A re-arrangement of the guns was effected. The number in the line was increased to 10 disposed as follows:— 6 guns in the front line; 2 in the close supports & 2 in the Strong Points. The 6 in Reserve were to occupy the Subsidiary line in case of attack. Two of these were used for indirect fire. This arrangement continued up till the end of April.	
	April		**General.** Except in the Subsidiary line the emplacements were in a dilapidated state, and a great deal of work had to be done in improving them and constructing new ones. Strong dug outs were non-existent & these were put in hand. Emplacements for Indirect fire were also constructed & used every night; the targets being the enemy's fire trenches; i.e. his 1st & Support lines; his C.T's, roads used by him & dumps. The guns in the front line fired about 2,000 rounds nightly at working parties &c. Two men were very slightly wounded by shell fire during April. Billets were good. Nothing else of interest occurred during April.	

C.J. Wiley Major

WAR DIARY or INTELLIGENCE SUMMARY

Army Form C. 2118

April — 51st Machine Gun Coy

Place	Date	Hour	Summary of Events and Information	Remarks and references to Appendices
ARMENTIERES	Apl. 4	11am	A re-distribution of the guns was effected; viz: 6 guns were placed in the front line and one in rear of the strong points.	
	19	11:30am	Two men, Ptes CORNELL and CLOSE slightly wounded by shell splinters.	
	N 20	"	Two more guns placed in the Support line; making 10 in all in the Brigade front. Two other guns reserved for Induced fire; leaving 4 guns in Billets for training purposes.	
	22	"	32 men from the Infy. attached for 3 weeks instruction to ensure the employment of = 12 guns in the line.	

General

During the month intensive fire at night was carried out from two specially constructed emplacements. "A" position was built in a house 2,300 yards in front of the German front line so that effective fire could be brought on his first & support lines & the corner trenches connecting them. Also on points from 500–600 yds in rear of his front. This fire apparently proved very effective the work was at once started in raising its parapet by two sand bags in depth. "B" emplacement was 1400 yds from the enemy's

WAR DIARY or INTELLIGENCE SUMMARY

51 M.G.C.

Army Form C. 2118

General (cont.)

front line from which fire was brought to bear on important points in his rear, such as dumps, C.T.s and roads used by ration parties &c. The extreme range was 2900 yds. The enemy artillery has been searching for these positions but they are so cunningly concealed that it is doubtful if he can ever discover them. The muzzle pivoting mountings we used for this indirect fire in conjunction with the dial elevator. An average of 2000 rounds a night is fired.

During the month work has been carried on in constructing a special type of emplacement in the front line & in holding very strong day "acts". The guns in the front line have done a lot of shooting with good effect at enemy working parties & also by indirect fire at important lines of commn. about 2000 to 2500 yds in rear of enemy's front line.

Godley Capt

WAR DIARY or INTELLIGENCE SUMMARY

Army Form C. 2118

51st Machine Gun Company Vol. 4

XVII

Place	Date	Hour	Summary of Events and Information	Remarks and references to Appendices
ARMENTIERES	May 6th	3 pm	Relief of one half company by the other half completed.	
"	13th	5 pm	Relieved by New Zealand Brigade.	
"	14th	11.45 pm	Left ARMENTIERES	
"	15	2.45 am	Arrived at ESTAIRES.	
"	15	2 pm	Left ESTAIRES.	
"	15	7.30 pm	Arrived MORBÉCQUE & billeted in the local school.	
"	16	10.15 am	Left MORBÉCQUE	
"	16	3.30 pm	Arrived WARDRECQUES & billeted in outbuildings of Convent.	
"	17	9.45 am	Left WARDRECQUES	
"	17	3.30 pm	Arrived PETIT DIFQUES about 8 miles N.W. of ST. OMER. During the march of about 50 miles no man fell out on the march; and 2 men only reported sick.	

WAR DIARY
or
INTELLIGENCE SUMMARY

Army Form C. 2118

51st Machine Gun Coy

Place	Date	Hour	Summary of Events and Information	Remarks and references to Appendices
ARMENTIERES			**General** — During the 1st half of May a great deal of useful work was done in the trenches. A new type of M.G. emplacement & strong dug out were built in the front line. Indirect fire was carried on every night. Otherwise nothing unusual occurred. Two Officers joined the Company during the month and 9 other ranks	
"	May 14	11.30 pm	2nd Lieut A.R. FRASER was slightly wounded.	
PETIT DI FRUSS	May 18 to 31st		The Company was engaged in intensive buildings. Billets in Bazino and satisfactory.	

Quincy Major
Commanding, 51 M.G.C.

51st Bde. Machine Gun Coy.

D.A.G.
 G.H.Q
  3 Echelon.

Herewith War Diary for June. Please ack. receipt hereon.

C.J. Wiley Major
Cmdg. 51 M. G. Coy.

13736.

WAR DIARY 51st Machine Gun Company
INTELLIGENCE SUMMARY for June 1916

Army Form C. 2118

Place	Date	Hour	Summary of Events and Information	Remarks and references to Appendices
ST. OMER	1-10	-	From 1st to 10th June the Company carried out training.	gpd
"	12	3 a.m.	Left Billets to entrain at St OMER for AMIENS. Without incident.	
ALLONVILLE	12	9.30 pm	Arrived in Billets at ALLONVILLE	
HEILLY	27	1 PM	Arrived after 4 hours march & went under Canvas.	
MORLANCOURT	30	12 PM M.N.	Arrived at MORLANCOURT to be ready to move in half an hour. On June 13th G.O.C. Divn asked me to work out a scheme for indirect fire during the preliminary Bombardment. This I had ready, emplacements & dug outs constructed by the 25th June. Four guns were used & during the 25th, 26th, 27th, 28th, 29th & 30th fired day & night an average of 10,000 rounds per gun daily. When the Artillery opened on the morning of the assault the guns also fired to an hour at a range of 2,900 yds & created a barrage of M.G. fire on an important point in rear of the enemy lines. The work done by these guns & then on 26th June there were 5 men wounded. Teams was very excellent.	

Apsley Major
Comdg 51st M.G. Coy.

51st Inf.Bde.
17th Div.

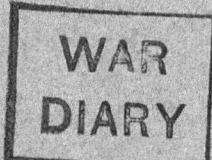

51st MACHINE GUN COMPANY.

J U L Y

1 9 1 6

WAR DIARY 51st Machine Gun Coy. Page 1 Army Form C. 2118
or
INTELLIGENCE SUMMARY for July 1916 Vol 6

(Erase heading not required.)

Place	Date	Hour	Summary of Events and Information	Remarks and references to Appendices
MORLAN-COURT	1.7.16	1 am	Arrived in Bellock as reserve to XV Corps.	
"	"	11:30 pm	Left Bellock & marched to near FRICOURT to relieve 50th Coy. Relief completed by 4 AM the 2nd. 8 guns placed in position in our old front line to go forward with attacking troops. 8 guns in rear for direct & indirect fire during the attack on FRICOURT on morning 2nd.	
FRICOURT	3.7.16	7:30 am	Attack held up in FRICOURT WOOD. All 16 guns taken forward to assist in pushing on the attack through the wood and on RAILWAY ALLEY. 12 guns were sent on & 4 kept in reserve in the wood. Attack succeeded & 10 guns went forward to held new line. Bottom Wood & SHELTER WOOD fell into our hands soon afterwards & when a line was being consolidated between these woods 4 guns were put into it, & in support about 600 yards back the other 8 kept in RAILWAY ALLEY for fire on QUADRANGLE TRENCH & MAMETZ WOOD.	
"	4.7.16	11 PM	Company was withdrawn to BILLETS at VILLE.	
VILLE	6.7.16	8 AM	Left VILLE & returned to the line. Relieved 52nd Coy that evening; ten guns being placed in QUADRANGLE TRENCH with advanced Infantry. 8 guns were employed in direct & indirect fire from RAILWAY ALLEY principally on MAMETZ WOOD; & 4 in Reserve at Hd Qrs in FRICOURT.	

Page 2

WAR DIARY 51st Machine Gun Coy
INTELLIGENCE SUMMARY for July 1916

(Erase heading not required.)

Army Form C. 2118.

Place	Date	Hour	Summary of Events and Information	Remarks and references to Appendices
FRICOURT	6.7.16	—	From the 6th to 10th July the Brigade was engaged in several attacks on QUADRANGLE SUPPORT and during this period fire was kept up day & night on the ground behind the enemy's lines. About 30,000 rounds were so expended. During the attack on CONTALMAISON on the 10th July 4 guns were sent forward to bring fire on the enemy retreating from it and to stop no reinforcements. These guns fired about 6,000 rounds during 2 hours. Total no. of rounds fired between 1st & 10th July was about 60,000. One Gun & Tripod was entirely destroyed by shell fire, one Tripod badly damaged, another Gun damaged Cross-head & 2 guns perforated by bullets. Casualties one man killed and 13 wounded by Shells.	
MEAULTE	11.7.16	4 am	arrived in BIVOUAC.	
FORDRINOY	12.7.16	1 am	" BILLETS after 14 miles march from Station at SALEUX.	
BUSSUS	14.7.16	5 pm	" BILLETS.	
BUIRE	23.7.16	11 pm	" BIVOUAC. & still here on 31.7.16	

C.P. Wiley Major
Comdg. 51 M.G. Coy.

51st Brigade.
17th Division.

51st BRIGADE MACHINE GUN COMPANY

AUGUST 1 9 1 6 ::

Confidential

WAR DIARY

51st. Machine Gun Company.

August 1916

WAR DIARY of the 37th Machine Gun Coy.
INTELLIGENCE SUMMARY for the month of August 1916.

Army Form C. 2118

(Erase heading not required.)

Place	Date	Hour	Summary of Events and Information	Remarks and references to Appendices
BUIRE	1/8/16	8 p.m.	Marched to POMMIER'S REDOUBT near MAMETZ arriving at 10.30 a.m. & relieved another Coy. taking its place as Supports	
MAMETZ	4/8/16	11 p.m.	10 guns arrived in DELVILLE WOOD in relief of 99th Coy. Their role was entirely defensive. Gun teams were relieved every 48 hours; each team on going in taking with it rations & water for that period. Intense heat prevailed & the route to the Wood was heavily shelled day & night. These guns were relieved on the night of 10 Aug. by 52 Coy. 2nd Lieut. C.F. BUSER was wounded on the 5th by Shrapnel. O.Rs. 2 killed & 8 wounded. No guns or other material lost. There was no attack during this period.	
"	12/8/16	10 a.m.	Withdrew in relief to BUIRE	
BUIRE	15/8/16	3 a.m.	Entrained for not Billets	
GÉZAINCOURT	"	3 p.m.	Arrived in BILLETS. marched next day to BEAUMAISON which was left on 18th for BIENVILLERS	
BIENVILLERS	20/8	—	Took over trenches from 168 Coy. 12 guns in trenches & 4 in Reserve. Usual trench work began such as reconstructing of emplacements, building new dugouts etc. positions as existing ones were very primitive.	
"	31/8	—	Nothing of importance to report, beyond 2 killed & 2 wounded on the 21st.	

Ogilvie Major
Comdg. 37 M.G. Coy

WAR DIARY of the 51st Machine Gun Coy

INTELLIGENCE SUMMARY

Army Form C. 2118

Vol 8

Place	Date	Hour	Summary of Events and Information	Remarks and references to Appendices
HANNESCAMP	1st – 11 Sept 1916	–	In trenches. Nothing of importance occurred. Relieved on 11th by 19th Coy.	
HALLOY	12"	–	Rested Billets at 3 a.m.	
BAYENCOURT	15"	–	Marched to BAYENCOURT. Billeted for night. Arrived at 7 p.m.	
HEBUTERNE	16	–	Took over in trenches from 50 Coy; 12 guns in line & 4 out	
	20	–	Relieved by 98th Coy	
HUMBERCAMP	20	–	Arrived about 4 p.m. & remained till 22nd	
DOULLENS	22	–	Marched from HUMBERCAMP to DOULLENS	
OUTREBOIS	23	–	Marched from DOULLENS to OUTREBOIS	
MAISON-PONTHIEU	24	–	" OUTREBOIS to MAISON PONTHIEU	
"	25–30	–	Training	

30.9.16

C Quiley Major
Comdg. 51 Machine Gun Coy.

Confidential

WAR DIARY

51st.

MACHINE GUN COMPANY

OCT. 1916.

WAR DIARY

INTELLIGENCE SUMMARY

51st Coy. M.G.C.

Army Form C. 2118

Place	Date	Hour	Summary of Events and Information	Remarks and references to Appendices
MAISON- PONTHIEU	28/9/16		Training.	
Left Maison PONTHIEU	1/10/16		Left Maison PONTHIEU to prepare for attack S. of GOMMERCOURT	
FROHON LE PETIT.	2/10/16		Stayed one night en route	
HALLOY	3/10/16			
BAYENCOURT	4/10/16			
HEBUTERNE	5/10/16		Took over line at HEBUTERNE. 12 guns in. 4 guns in Reserve.	
SOUASTRE	14/10/16		Relieved by 50 Coy M.G.C. & marched to billets in SOUASTRE.	
LUCHEUX.	19/10/16		Left SOUASTRE and marched to LUCHEUX.	
TREUX.	22/10/16		Left LUCHEUX at 1.30 pm on 22/10/16 & travelled to TREUX by motor lorry. Transport left on 21-10-16 marching by road & arrived 22-10-16.	
CITADEL	27/10/16		Left TREUX and marched to CITADEL.	
E.TRANSLOY LINE N.28 & 34	31/10/16		Left Citadel at 9.5.am 31/10/16 & marched to MONTAUBAN and ay moved to line de TRANSLOY relieving 25.M.g. Coy with 16 guns.	

Vereur Goss Lieut
OC 51 M.G. Coy

WAR. DIARY.
of.
51st Machine Gun Coy.
for November. 1916.
VOLUME. I.

WAR DIARY
or
INTELLIGENCE SUMMARY
(Erase heading not required.)

Army Form C. 2118

Place	Date	Hour	Summary of Events and Information	Remarks and references to Appendices
N.28. Sheet 57c 20.10.0	1-11-16	11 a.m.	Completed relieving the 25th M.G. Coy. with 16 guns. Distribution of guns: Eight in front line four in support, four in reserve.	
N.28.a, 8.9 to N.28.c.6.4.5.	3-11-16	after noon	On the 3-11-16 the Enemy attempted to bombard our lines and delivered an attack on the right of the front held by the Brigade. Four guns, two of which were situated in a sap at the right end of MISTY TRENCH N.28.c.8.9.; the other two in GUSTY TRENCH N.28.c.1.7. fired effectively on the Enemy. The attack was beaten off.	
From N.28. Sheet 57c to A.8.a.8.2.	8 = 11-16		Eight guns & teams were withdrawn to H. Camp A.8.a.8.2. for rest.	
C. Camp S.23.b.5.3.	12-11-16		One section of four guns was relieved by the 1st Guards Bde. M.G. Coy. & moved to C. Camp S.23.b.5.3.	
C. Camp S.23.b.5.3.	13-11-16		One section of four guns was relieved by the 3rd Guards Bde. M.G. Coy. & moved to C. Camp S.23.b.5.3. The Casualties received in killed & wounded during the period from 1-11-16 to 13-11-16. Officers 1. O.R.S. wounded O.R. 6.	
H. Camp to MEAULTE.	"		Two sections of the Company moved from H. Camp & A.8.a.8.2. to MEAULTE.	
C. Camp to MANSEL Camp	14-11-16	5 pm	Two sections of the Company moved from C. Camp to MANSEL Camp P.M.R.	
MANSEL Camp to MEAULTE	15-11-16		Two sections of the Company moved from MANSEL Camp to MEAULTE.	

51st Machine Gun Company.

Army Form C. 2118

WAR DIARY
or
INTELLIGENCE SUMMARY
(Erase heading not required.)

Place	Date	Hour	Summary of Events and Information	Remarks and references to Appendices
MEAULTE to Divisional Rest Area.	15-11-16		Transport moved with Divisional Train from MEAULTE to the Divisional Rest Area by road.	
MEAULTE to SOUES.	16-11-16		The Company marched from MEAULTE to Edgehill Station DERNACOURT and entrained at 11 am for Divisional Rest Area. Arrived at HANGEST at 6 pm. Marched from HANGEST to billets at SOUES arriving at 7.30 pm.	
SOUES.	17-11-16 to 30-11-16		Reorganizing and Equipping the Company. Training was carried out at the rate of four to five hours a day.	

P. Manufuntiu Lieut
for o/c 51 M.G Coy.

29-11-16

Army Form C. 2118

51st M.G. Coy.

Vol XI

WAR DIARY or INTELLIGENCE SUMMARY
(Erase heading not required.)

Place	Date	Hour	Summary of Events and Information	Remarks and references to Appendices
SOUES	1/12/16 11/12/16		Reorganising & re-equipping the Company. Training was carried out at the rate of 4 hours to two hours a day.	
SOUES to CORBIE	18/12/16		The Company marched from SOEUS to HANGEST and entrained at 9.20 a.m. for CORBIE. Arrived CORBIE at 10.15 p.m. Transport marched by road arriving at 6 p.m.	
CORBIE	13/12/16 22/12/16		The Company continued Training.	
CORBIE to MEAULTE	23/12/16		The Company, with Transport, marched to MEAULTE, being CORBIE at 9 a.m. and passing through MERICOURT and TREUX. Arrived MEAULTE 12.15 p.m.	
MEAULTE to CAMP 20, CARNOY EAST	24/12/16		The Company, with Transport, marched from MEAULTE to CAMP 20, CARNOY EAST via FRICOURT and MAMETZ. Leaving MEAULTE at 9 a.m. and arriving at CAMP 20 at 11.45 a.m.	
CAMP 20 CARNOY E.	25/12/16		The Company moved from CAMP 20, CARNOY EAST to MANSEL CAMP, F.11.b.	
MANSEL CAMP F.11.b.	26/12/16			
MANSEL CAMP to CAMPS 18 & 21 CARNOY E.	30/12/16		Three Sections of the Company moved from MANSEL CAMP, F.11.b. to Camps 18 & 21 CARNOY EAST.	
CAMPS 18 & 21 CARNOY E. to GUILLEMONT	31/12/16		At 8 a.m. two 1/4 Sections GUILLEMONT where they met Guides and Carried out reliefs of 2 Sections of the 50th M.G. Coy in Trenches THISTLE, CONN & OX (Central) (T.3, Central) At 10.30 a.m. the 3 Section moved from Camps 18 & 21 CARNOY EAST to Cotters Post Line. 2 guns E. ZENITH TRENCH (N.34.9.9.) and 2 guns in AUTUMN and FALL TRENCHES. (N.95.C. Cent.)	

1875 Wt. W593/826 1,000,000 4/15 J.B.C. & A. A.D.S.S./Forms/C. 2118.

WAR DIARY or INTELLIGENCE SUMMARY

Army Form C. 2118

Place	Date	Hour	Summary of Events and Information	Remarks and references to Appendices
MANSEL CAMP 18/11/16 to Camp 18 & 21 CARNOY E. and GUILLEMONT	18/11/16		The remainder of the Company moved from MANSEL CAMP to Camps 18 & 21 CARNOY EAST. Camps and Wood quarters taken over from 2/8 502 no 5 Coy 1/5	For Pardew Lieut O/c. 5. n/ Coy

WAR DIARY / INTELLIGENCE SUMMARY

Army Form C. 2118

51st MacRae Gun Coy.

51 M G Coy

Vol 12

Place	Date	Hour	Summary of Events and Information	Remarks and references to Appendices
	1-1-17		The 6th Australian Machine Gun Coy took over 6 of our guns namely 2 in Bart's Tr H.34.b, 2 in Bristol Tr H.34.c & 2 in Carl Tr 7.3.a. The Bar Sub 7.8.a.	
	5-1-17		The 51st M.G. Coy took over 6 guns from the 52nd M.G. Coy namely:- 2 in Bennett Tr 7.5.b, 2 in Bead Tr 7.5.c and 2 in Ox Tr. 7.9.b. There was a bombardment by our artillery of the German front line. During the barrage our guns carried out indirect fire.	
	6-1-17		A direct fire gun was carried out on the night of the 6/7 Jan the Bigot's Bend & Tramway and Cemetery Circle H.30.d and H.36.b. The batts were fired upon.	
	7-1-17		Direct fire was carried out on the night of the 7/8 Jan. The Bigot's Bend & Tramway and Cemetery Circle. Word had been received that a German relief was about to take place with 500 rounds were fired.	
	8-1-17		One gun was withdrawn from Autumn Tr H.35.c. Being only 3 guns in the front line. Another Bar Bar was again. Table one gun The 50th M.G. Coy & Webster Tr 7.6.a.	
	9-1-17		Another gun was received in a German relief was to take place on the night of the 9/10 Jan. Consequently in order to harass the... 48 mins as possible indirect fire was carried out & 4 guns on the Tramway and Cemetery Circle. 1000 rounds were fired from each gun off the fixed lines. Long Le Tramway and	
	10-1-17		Cemetery Circle. 1000 rounds were fired.	
	11-1-17		One of the guns in Bead Tr again fired 1000 rounds indirect on Le Tramway and Cemetery Circle. The gun in Carnoy Camp moved up to man the Tr at Guillemont, and on 15 of the 183. Tumblebury Coy this man became the new position but the man out the Bar.	
	12-1-17		It accordingly went the 249 relieve 1000 rounds were along a 100 in the afternoon from the gun in Bead Tr again.	
	13-1-17		The gun in Bead Tr again fired 1000 rounds indirect on Le Tramway and Cemetery Circle.	
	15-1-17		The gun at 1.80p.m. The night of the 12/13 Jan the 51st M.G. Coy were relieved in the Tr by the 6th Aus M.G. Coy at 8.00. The relief of the 52nd Bar Bart guns the Bennet Lincoln and Webster Trenches was by the Bars at 9.40 p.m. Coy at 9.40 p.m. The Coy was completed returned to Bde Cpt. during the turn in the trenches cash was incurred. One cartridge was needed yet.	

Lesbœufs Sector

51st Machine Gun Company (contd.)

Army Form C. 2118

WAR DIARY
or
INTELLIGENCE SUMMARY
(Erase heading not required.)

Instructions regarding War Diaries and Intelligence Summaries are contained in F. S. Regs., Part II. and the Staff Manual respectively. Title Pages will be prepared in manuscript.

Place	Date	Hour	Summary of Events and Information	Remarks and references to Appendices
Camp 21 CARNOY	15-1-17		After relief the Coy. moved to Camp 21 CARNOY EAST and stayed the night there.	
CARNOY to MEAULTE	16-1-17		The Coy. moved by road from Camp 21 CARNOY EAST to MEAULTE. The original intention was to go to TREOX but no billets being found there the Coy was billeted in MEAULTE instead. By CARNOY main.	
MEAULTE	17-1-17 to 23-1-17		The Coy. trained, was re-equipped and reorganised at MEAULTE.	
MEAULTE to BRONFAY FARM	24-1-17		The Coy. with Transport moved from MEAULTE to BRONFAY FARM. CAMP 108 F.8.9.a. via BRAY.	
BRONFAY FARM to MALTZ HORN	25-1-17		The Coy moved by road from BRONFAY FARM F.8.9.a to MALTZ HORN A.6.a passing through MARICOURT and HARDECOURT.	
MALTZ HORN T.23.b.5.3	27-1-17		The Coy relieved the 60th M.G. Coy. in the line. 6 gun teams relieved 9 coys in Bn Coy. H.Q. T.23.b.5.3. Positions X1, T.18.a.0.6, X2, T.18.c.8.8.1, W1, V.14.a.0.8, W4, V.17.c.5.9. 10 gun teams relieved Bn HQRS in Sally SAILLISEL arc positions U1, V.14.a.9.6, U2, V.8.c.6.0.0.3, U3, V.8.c.7.5, U4, V.8.c.9.8.0, V1, V.8.a.7.2, V2, V.8.a.6.4, V3, V.8.a.5.5, V4, V.8.c.5.9, W2, V.7.a.5.4, W3, V.7.b.6.0. Coy HQ. at T.23.b.5.3. Relief complete at 9 p.m.	
T.23.b.5.3.	28-1-17 to 31-1-17		In the line.	

Maurice Parker Lieut
O.C. 51st Machine Gun Coy

31-1-17

51st Bty. Machine Gun Corps

Army Form C. 2118

WAR DIARY
INTELLIGENCE SUMMARY
(Erase heading not required.)

Vol 13

Place	Date	Hour	Summary of Events and Information	Remarks and references to Appendices
	1-2-17		There was a bombardment by our artillery in which 8 of our guns took part. Targets as follows (a) Brunswick tr. (b) Gotha tr. (c) Wagner tr. Our firing commenced at 10.30 p.m. and lasted till 12.31 p.m. Between 1 p.m. and 1.30 p.m. an enemy aeroplane flew very low over our positions spotting for the bosch guns. No machine gun fire was brought to bear on this plane. Our teams during this time lay still. Enemy retaliation was very effective.	
	2-2-17		At 2 a.m. W4 was moved to Stag Pt U.7.b. At 6 a.m. V8 was moved back to U.8.a.4.8.5. At 2 p.m. V4 was moved to U.8.c.4.9.2. There was a bombardment by our artillery in which 8 of our guns participated. Our guns fired from 7.18.d.6.0 (a.b.c.) and are from U.13.b.88. At 2 p.m. the second gun from T.18.a.8.0 opened fire on enemy trench from U.13.b.88. Also guns at U.13.b.88 fired at tr. road and an road at U.10.d. 18/9.0. Gun at 7.18.a.80 fired on trench mortar bay gr. U.7. Leading from the front line to BAYREUTH tr. The second gun fired at the same pt. The Boche gun teams flying fire was to other side of front line to this gr. The gun at U.13.b.88 was heavy bombarding about 3.30 p.m. enemy planes were our back positions. This account of not greatly some being got at U.13.b. Before the bombing at night these planes were flying very low and had fired on a gun also come over to a no and the Boche bomb gr. and did not come very well. No fire was brought on our planes. Two guns at T.18.c.8.0 fired on the bombing targets at a U13 bridge. Very little retalitation to our fire from 10 a.m. to 10 p.m. This was done to very slight.	
	3-2-17		6 p.m. at U.7.b. There was also coming out from the country at U.13.b.8.8. 10 p.m. at S.P. in order to pass on any info that came to late places that were T.18.a.80 PRAGUE tr. U.3.b V MS.a.0 CORPSE GALLIA tr. U.3.b LOON CORPSE GALLIA tr from 100 coord
	4-2-17		At 2 a.m. to assist in a bombardment 9 of our battery guns fired on parties T.18.a.80. Targets were (a) BRUNSWICK tr. U.8.b (b) WAGNER U.8.d (c) GOTHA tr. (e) C.P.C.

51st Coy. Machine Gun Corps

WAR DIARY
INTELLIGENCE SUMMARY
(Erase heading not required.)

Army Form C. 2118

Place	Date	Hour	Summary of Events and Information	Remarks and references to Appendices
	6-2-17		Firing lasted from 12 noon to 1 p.m. 2500 rounds was fired	
	8-2-17		The 14th Division was ordered to attack and capture the general front line of objects. The B.Coy on a basis from O.14.b.65.05. to V.15.c.05.70 with a view to supporting the Bed. and SAILLY SAILLISEL and along in the enemy's counter attack from V.13 central and T.18.d. The attack was carried out by B.Coy named the 7th Yorkshire Regt. The 1st Coy of 20th CUSHY, CHATEAU, and SOUTH CORPS were reinforced for the attack. The Coy was ordered to go ahead with the central machine gun fire for 4 guns a teatres from V.14.b.36 a the line of Tank Copse V.15.b.4.y to V.19.c.60. Indirect fire position were chosen at V.14.b.04 lines of fire in each gun. Stops of water. The position were marked and obtaining effective fire. The guns were from V.15.b.40.40 – V.15.b.05.70 – V.13.a.90.90 V.13.a.90.90. V.15.a.65.95. 104." to guns from V.15.a.65.95. – V.15.a.90.90 – U.9.c.35".20 There was about of the 300 Bn of Gas attack and machine gun and rifle fire for 3 hr on Reid. There was no following bombardment by our artillery. In a sweeping range of 6. During our making our fires there was a constant amount of hostile shelling also to guns. Goy employed under very active as equ and even apparent at very low attitude over the guns. At 5:30 p.m. the enemy commenced an intense bombardment a met our attack on the advance by post of this Line. Beams no part the position would be evacuated. The teams took by the stop part of U.7.6 in SAILLY SAILLISEL were fired for 4 hours in 6 days between 9 am at 8.30 p.m. and the bombardment of the was fired up and commenced on an own S.O.S. barrage fired at the enemy's lines the coy the gun and sup SAILLY SAILLISEL and CHATEAU WOOD were barrage fired and exp morning	
	9-2-17		The 4 guns which Red accompanied the indirect task of new position taken of NORTH CORPS U.7.d.07. to O.0b to c.00 to fire at the same angle, shelling occasion arose	

31st Coy. M.G.C.

WAR DIARY
INTELLIGENCE SUMMARY
(Erase heading not required.)

Army Form C. 2118

Place	Date	Hour	Summary of Events and Information	Remarks and references to Appendices
Q	9-2-17		Communication was maintained. G.O. nights of the HESSULE at night by M.O. Patrol. Everything was correct.	
"	10-2-17		G.O.4 relieved the guns - resumed ordinary routine at 10.45 p.m. in CHATEAU WOOD	
"	11-2-17		8 for guns on SAILLY-SAILLISEL were relieved at dawn by 8 teams of the 50th M.G. Coy. and proceeded to billets at BRONFAY FARM.	
"	13-2-17		At 6 a.m. they were again taken over by the 8 gun in CHATEAU WOOD. Our Coy. place also 8 teams. The guns on the road were taken up to Paris Redt. by 13 teams, nil casualties. Our 8 teams proceeded east of SAILLY SAILLISEL. 8 teams reported to Rgt. HQ. CHATEAU WOOD from 3pm - 4pm.	
7.23.6.53	14-2-17		8 Back guns were relieved by 8 guns of 50th M.G.C. Our Coy relieved the guns of M2, M3, M4 with relief was completed by 7.15 p.m. 8 teams and Coy HQ under B. Capt. 8 teams and Brigade HQ were taken at 7.20 p.m.	
7.23.6.53 to BRONFAY FARM			Coy was carried from 10.20 partridges anti-tanks during our tour in the line.	
—	15-2-17		1 man evacuated Coy. was taken with draft by subaltern to baths. Impector.	
BRONFAY FARM	16-2-17 1-3-17		Coy. wrote Dept. Tea F.D.Q. BRONFAY to Ten. The usual Bn. inspection. Coy received order to move to BUSSY & held itself ready to go forward, Not marched up in order owing to P.D. Pontoons.	
BRONFAY to FLESSELLES	19-2-17		CO Cap. Potter walked 4 guns. Proceeded to FLESSELLES to select a rest field Coy went this date. At Plateau Farm at 8.30 p.m.	
BRONFAY to FLESSELLES	20-2-17		Marched to FLESSELLES arriving Flo at 80 men. The Bn Coy was among AMIENS 8 am. Y	
FLESSELLES to FRANVILLERS			Coy. marched from BRONFAY FARM to FRANVILLERS via BRAY, MORCOURT VILLE TREUX MERICOURT, HEILLY. Being BRONFAY 9.0 am. among FRANVILLERS 3.30 pm.	
FRANVILLERS to BUSSY LES DAOURS	21-2-17		Coy. marched from FRANVILLERS to BUSSY LES DAOURS was POST No. 74628 and QUERRIEU being FRANVILLERS 10 am. among BUSSY 12.30 pm.	
BUSSY	22-2-17 to 28-2-17		Coy. Trained was inspected and reported at BUSSY.	

The Batn at FLESSELLES was billeted ?? and ??
P. Hodge Major
O.C. 31 M.G. Coy.
1875 Wt. W593/826 1,000,000 4/15 J.B.C. & A. A.D.S.S./Forms/C. 2118.

Vol/14

WAR DIARY.

VOLUME. I.
of
51st MACHINE GUN COMPANY.
for
MARCH. 1917.

Original Copy.

Addressed.
 H. Qrs. 51st Infantry Bde.

Army Form C. 2118.

WAR DIARY
INTELLIGENCE SUMMARY

51st Machine Gun Company.

Original Copy.

(Erase heading not required.)

Instructions regarding War Diaries and Intelligence Summaries are contained in F.S. Regs., Part II. and the Staff Manual respectively. Title pages will be prepared in manuscript.

Place	Date	Hour	Summary of Events and Information	Remarks and references to Appendices
BUSSY-LES-DAOURS.	1-3-17		The Company continued training the Company.	
RUBEMPRÉ.	2-3-17		The 17th Division from the 14th Corps - 4th Army to the 5th Army. Marching from Bussy to RUBEMPRÉ. Route: Bussy, Pont Noyelles, Behencourt, Bavelincourt, Beaucourt sur L'Halhie.	
"	3-3-17		The Company recommenced training.	
"	5-3-17		Two gun teams were dispatched to PUSHEVILLERS on anti-aircraft duty to guard railhead dump.	
"	12-3-17		The two anti-aircraft teams rejoined the Company.	
LONGUEVIL-LETTE	13-3-17		The Company marched to LONGUEVILLETTE. Route: TALMAS - CANDAS - FIENVILLERS. (Route: FIENVILLERS - BERNAVILLE - BEAUMETZ - AGENVILLE - CONTEVILLE - to MAISON-PONTHIEU.)	
NEUILLY LE DIEN.	14-3-17		Company marched from LONGUEVILLETTE to NEUILLY LE DIEN.	
CHÉRIENNE	15-3-17		The Company marched to CHÉRIENNE. Route: AQUEST, AUXI-le-CHATEAU, LE PONCHEL, GENNE-MERGNY, LA BROYE, REGNAUVILLE, CHÉRIENNE.	
"	16-3-17 to 21-3-17		The Company commenced training & continued until 21-3-17	
MAMUR FARM. (BUIRE AU BOIS.)	22-3-17		The Company moved to MAMUR FARM. (BUIRE AU BOIS.) Route: FONTAINE L'ETALON, QUOEUX, HARTAVESNES, BACHIMONT, BUIRE AU BOIS.	

Army Form C. 2118

51st Machine Gun Company.

WAR DIARY
or
INTELLIGENCE SUMMARY

(Erase heading not required.)

Original Copy.

Place	Date	Hour	Summary of Events and Information	Remarks and references to Appendices
BREVILLERS.	23-3-17	—	The Company marched to BREVILLERS. Route HOEUX, WAVANS, FROHEN LE GRAND, REMAISNIL, NEUVILLETTE, BOUQUEMAISON.	
OPPY.	24-3-17		The Company marched from BREVILLERS to OPPY passing through IVERGNY, BEAUDRICOURT.	
"	26-3-17 to 31-3-17		The Company continued training.	

W. Gardner Capt.

WAR DIARY or INTELLIGENCE SUMMARY

Army Form C. 2118.

57th/R.9 Coy

Jul 15

Place	Date	Hour	Summary of Events and Information	Remarks and references to Appendices
	1/4/17		Officer reinforcement for the Coy Lt. F.S. Wilson. Coy continued training. Weather snow.	
	2/4/17		Snowy. Coy continued Weather. More snow. Brigade scheme.	
	3/4/17		Orders received for move to BUNEVILLE Area. Preparations made accordingly.	
	4/4/17		Coy left OPPY at 8.10 a.m. Transport marched in rear of the Company Route: IVERGNY – REU VIETTE – HOUVIN – MONCHEAUX. Arrived in billets at BUNÉVILLE at 1.4 p.m.	
	6/4/17		Training and packing once unpacking finished.	
	7/4/17		The Company marched out of BUNÉVILLE area to LIGNEREUIL leaving Buneville at 10.30 a.m. arriving at 1.00 p.m.	
	8/4/17		Company marched from LIGNEREUIL to LATTRE ST QUENTIN. Leaving at 9.40 a.m. arriving 1.00 p.m. Route GIVENCHY – LE-NOBLE – MANIN – NOY-VION. Company drew 2 sandbags per man, one bomb per man, one rifle per man, and two days emergency rations. Enemy aeroplane flew over Brigade whilst on the march.	
	9/4/17		Zero day for attack on ARRAS front. Zero was at 5 a.m. Company came at Ronville from 3 a.m. to 4 a.m. and at 4.45 a.m. hours notice from ZTG Arras road. Route HABARQ to AUBIGNY. Bivouacked on road at 10.30 p.m. about three kilometres	

A5834 Wt. W4973/M687 750,000 8/16 D.D. & L. Ltd. Forms/C.2118/13.

WAR DIARY
or
INTELLIGENCE SUMMARY.
(Erase heading not required.)

Army Form C. 2118.

Place	Date	Hour	Summary of Events and Information	Remarks and references to Appendices
	10/4/17		Short of Arras. Considerable snowfall of snow during the night. Company moved off again at about 9.30 am. and marched into billets in Arras, arriving about 12.45 pm. Snow continues.	
	11/4/17		Remained in billets at Arras at lay on hour notice.	
	12/4/17		Received orders to move into area occupied by 46th Infantry Brigade, at Railway Triangle H.19 Central. Party went on to take over accommodation. Snow continues.	
	13/4/17		Company moved off at 6.45 am from Arras to Railway Triangle arriving at 9.20 am. Two guns remained with company for A.A. duty. Remainder proceeded to FEUCHY G.22.6.6.4.	
	14/4/17		Capt Gardner and four Section Officers proceeded to 88th M.G. Coy. HdQrs near Feuchy Chapel N.J.B. preparatory to taking over line at MONCHY-LE-PREUX at 4 pm. Heavy barrage put down by enemy at Monchy-le-Preux and NORTHWARDS to the Scarpe. Enemy attempted to attack about 4.30 pm from Bois-du-SART. O.J.B. Their leading waves were broken up by our barrage. Relief with 88th M.G. Coy arranged for 11-6 pm. but was suspended at 9.0 pm and finally cancelled. Remained at Railway Triangle.	
	15/4/17			
	16/4/17		Orders received for eight guns to join junction to bring personnel for	

WAR DIARY or INTELLIGENCE SUMMARY

Army Form C. 2118

Place	Date	Hour	Summary of Events and Information	Remarks and references to Appendices
	17/4/17		Men on cross roads at I.25.D. Positions chosen at N.6.A.2.H. Guns from Feuchy region Company. Nos 1 & 2 Sections proceed at dusk to N.6.A.2.H. to dig positions. Returned same night.	
	18/4/17		Nos 1 & 2 Sections move up to N.6.A.2.H. taking guns on pack animals. Remainder of Company prepared to move to BROWN LINE (ORANGE HILL). Company move off at 5.30 a.m. along railway to Feuchy and from there along Feuchy – Fampoux road. Company Hd. Qrs. formed H.28.C.57 at 5 a.m. Company Hd. Qrs. move to Feuchy at mid-day. Nos 3 & 4 Sections relieved out of Brown Line by 50th M.G. Coy and relieve two Sections of 52nd M.G. Coy in Monchy le Preux. Two guns remain at Coy Hd. Qtrs in Monchy. Positions remain unchanged. Eight guns at N.6.A.2.H. relieved by 8 guns of 52nd M.G. Coy and in turn relieve eight guns of 50th M.G. Coy on gun pits at H.29.B.5.8.	
	20/4/17		Positions remain unchanged.	
	21/4/17 22/4/17		Orders received for attack on the 23rd. A general advance along the whole line. Divisions interval 51st in the left, 17th centre, 29th on the right. 14th Division, 51st Brigade will attack 50th in support, 52nd	

WAR DIARY or INTELLIGENCE SUMMARY

Army Form C. 2118

Place	Date	Hour	Summary of Events and Information	Remarks and references to Appendices
	23/4/17		on recent Objectives 4th Border Trench System L 35 & L 25 C and Blue LINE 8th South Staffords Trench System L 25 C and Blue Line. 10th Sherwoods in support to 4th Borders. 7th Lincolns in support to 8th South Staffs. Four guns 57th M.G. Coy in Brigade Reserve push forward to ypres and L 21 Central to barrage same leading into PERNES. L 26 D. Second phase 10th Sherwoods attack Kuiling Copse. 7th Lincolns attack Pelves. from the west. See R.u.48a.m. 23/4/17. Report on Operations. According to plan that two Bos of 51st Brigade attacked on sub-section of two Guns was sent forward with each Bn, the plan being for them to consolidate when objectives were reached. The attack being under cover. The guns came into action on several targets to the flanks during this period one gun team was knocked out and Pt. A.S. Welsh killed. Two more teams were attached to the two supporting Bats and did good work. The agits guns of No 122 Section in prepared positions at H.29.B. 5.8 assisted the attack by firing from Z to Z+15 min on to rear of German lines. Rate of fire about six box per gun.	

WAR DIARY or INTELLIGENCE SUMMARY

Army Form C. 2118

(Erase heading not required.)

Place	Date	Hour	Summary of Events and Information	Remarks and references to Appendices

These guns then came into Brigade Reserve in readiness to go forward to Kurban further inland. Her position of attack was successful. Fisher Park Mules were kept close behind in open in H.29.C. to bring up A.A. etc forward. Our troops having made very little progress, this plan was abandoned and the guns were in on a defensive line in the ridge behind Lone Copse Sale Roy were withdrawn to their original positions. Lewis gun officers 1/6 O. and men did their work splendidly and untiringly and I must specially mention 2/L. S.G. Arnold who after taking his own two guns over to Lone Copse found a Company of Infantry without officers and took charge of them. 2/L. A.C. Forshaw also did good work throughout the time. 2/L. L.S. Nelson killed 2/L. J.B. Pyle wounded, 2/L. L.C. Tipple wounded, other ranks killed fourteen, wounded [?]

24/4/1917 1.15 am The Company was relieved by 501 M.G. Co. early morning about 1.15 am and withdrawn to dug-outs in Railway triangle.

Army Form C. 2118

WAR DIARY
or
INTELLIGENCE SUMMARY
(Erase heading not required.)

Instructions regarding War Diaries and Intelligence Summaries are contained in F.S. Regs., Part II. and the Staff Manual respectively. Title Pages will be prepared in manuscript.

Place	Date	Hour	Summary of Events and Information	Remarks and references to Appendices
	25/4/17		Company moved to BEAUDRICOURT entraining at Arras station detraining at SAULTY. The transport moved by road.	
	26/4/17 to 30/4/17		Rest. Reorganising and re-equipping the Company. Reinforcements arrived during this period 37 other ranks.	2nd Lt Robertson went to OC 51st Machine Gun Company 2-5-17.

WAR DIARY
or
INTELLIGENCE SUMMARY
(Erase heading not required.)

Army Form C. 2118.

51st M.G. Coy

Place	Date	Hour	Summary of Events and Information	Remarks and references to Appendices
Beaudricourt to Y. Hut	1/5/17		Coy moved from Beaudricourt to Y hut N.S.6. by motor bus arriving at 5.30 p.m.	
	2/5/17		Remained in Y Hut	
	3/5/17		Moved to St Nicholas Camp G.17 & 3.7 arriving about 10 a.m.	
	4/5/17 5/5/17		Remained in St Nicholas Camp	
	9/5/17		Four Sections left about 7 p.m. to dig indirect fire positions at H.11.B.9.7 returned early morning of 10/5/17	
	10/5/17		Fourteen Guns Section left to inverst fire positions at 8 p.m. preparatory to attacks on night of 11th early morning of 12th	
	11/5/17		Attack by 51st Division on Chemical Works Zero 7.30 p.m. Fourteen Guns Cooperated Targets I.13.B.49 to I.8.C.04 and I.8.4.00 & I.2.Coo Guns ceased fire Z + 30. Further action from Section Guns started between these limits throughout the night.	
	12/5/17		A conjunction with 4th Div 17th Bn attacked line CURLY, CHARLIE, TRENCHES. 152nd Brigade attacked Zero 6.30 a.m. Fourteen Guns cooperated on following targets I.17.D.65.00 to I.8.C.09 & I.8.4.00 & I.2.Coo - Nature of fire rapid to Z + 12 from lift of 200 yards from Zero to cease fire Z + 90. Further action fire concentrated on Railway Cutting between I.14.B & I.8.C.11 for remainder of day.	

WAR DIARY or INTELLIGENCE SUMMARY.

Army Form C. 2118.

(Erase heading not required.)

Place	Date	Hour	Summary of Events and Information	Remarks and references to Appendices
	13/5/17		Guns remained in position laid on S.O.S. lines during day - night of 13/14	
	14/5/17		Guns withdrawn, returned to St NICHOLAS.	
	15/5/17		Remained St NICHOLAS. Company relieved Guns of 52 & 53 Companies in line - Positions :- 3 Guns in CUBA T. I.7.D.5.O - 2 North of junction CUT - CUBA - 1 South of same + 1 in CASH T. + 1 at I.I.C.6.I. 1 at I.I.D.O.2. - 4 Guns in HOLLY T. H.II.T2. - 6 Guns HAWTHORN T. H.6.C. - Guns in HAWTHORN, HOLLY, barrage guns - Targets Cross Roads I.D.C. joins S.E. of GREENLAND HILL.	
	16/5/17	1.30.a.m.	Relief complete. Enemy attack take CUPID T. I.14.t. Our guns out of action in CASH T. This gun replaced immediately. Guns in HOLLY T. relieved by 52 M.G. Coy & come into Brigade Reserve. Guns in HAWTHORN Change position to HUSSAR T. Five Guns cooperate with 33rd Div. attack on HAWTHORN T. C.25.A-B. Targets C.25.D.95.00 & C.25.D.50.95.	
	17/5/17			
	18/5/17		Company Headquarters moved from Sunken R^d A.II.A.6.I. to PUDDING T. H.IO.D. Into Company relief. Night of 18/19th	

T2134. Wt. W708—776. 500000. 4/15. Sir J. C. & S.

WAR DIARY
or
INTELLIGENCE SUMMARY.
(Erase heading not required.)

Army Form C. 2118.

Place	Date	Hour	Summary of Events and Information	Remarks and references to Appendices
	19/5/17		One Gun in HULST T. Put out of action. Position for 2 Guns prepared in CAZABAR T.17.B.45. A-A positions prepared in CAZADAR T.17.4.7.2. Two Guns take up positions in CAZADAR T. Two defensive positions commenced in CREED T.H.18 A.19 + 1.10. AA position in CASS T.	
	20/5/17			
	21/5/17		Finished Gun damaged on 16th in action again. Two Guns teams moved into CREED T.	
	22/5/17		New Guns received to replace Guns damaged on 9th. One thousand rounds fired on tracks in vicinity of GREENLAND HILL night of 21/22. Enemy MG reported at last I.7.D.4.8. I.7.D.4.5. I.7.D.50.65.	
	23/5/17		One Thousand rounds fired on Cross Roads I.2.C. Attack in vicinity Into company relief for front line teams. Dig outs in CAZABAR + CREED T. finished.	
night of 23/24			Intermittent firing on enemy tracks at GREENLAND HILL.	
	25/5/17		Into Company relief for front line teams. Two Guns relieve two Guns of 38 M.G.Coy. at I.1.C.98.00 + I.1.C.80.30.	
night of 25/26	26/5/17		Reinforcements relieved from us by 50 M.G.Coy on 26/5/17.	

WAR DIARY
or
INTELLIGENCE SUMMARY.
(Erase heading not required.)

Army Form C. 2118.

Place	Date	Hour	Summary of Events and Information	Remarks and references to Appendices
	26/5/17		Night of 26th. Raid by 8th South Staffs. Object to raid posts in CHAPLIN NOOK of CAPH, enemy's strong point at junction of CURLY & CAPH T. Returning to our lines via CAPH T. destroying tombing post west of junction CAPH - CURLY - Two guns via CAPH co-operated by keeping enemy's heads down in CHARLIE T. ZERO 12.58 a.m.	
	27/5/17 28/5/17		Nothing of importance - Guns very heavily shelled withdrawn out of CARRER TRENCH. One team tried. Four guns take up position in CADIZ T. One of this being withdrawn from CROA T. Begin from CALMAR T & two from CREED T.	
	29/5/17 30/5/17		Gave fir relief night of 30/31 by 34 M.G. Coy. NCOs men of 101st M.G. Coy came into line early morning to learn positions. Relief commenced 9.15 p.m. from Coy H.Q. completed 1.30 a.m.	
	31/5/17		Company returned to S. NICHOLAS CAMP. Entrained to an. in KESTYKEN transport by road. Arrive POMMERA near DOULLENS about 1 p.m. Transport arrive about 3 p.m.	

M. Barrow Capt.
O/C 57th M.G. Coy

57th Machine Gun Company

61 MG Coy
Vol 17

WAR DIARY
or
INTELLIGENCE SUMMARY

Army Form C. 2118.

Place	Date	Hour	Summary of Events and Information	Remarks and references to Appendices
Pommera to Sailly	1-6-17		The Company was in training at Pommera from the 1-6-17 to 22-6-17. On the 1st and 4 guns were sent to Sailly to help our Anti-aircraft positions from the M.G. Coy.	
Pommera to St Nicholas Camp.	9-6-17 22-6-17		4 guns at Sailly relieved by 50. MG Coy & returned to Pommera. The Bde moved by bus to St Nicholas Camp G.17.c.5.7. Transport by road proceeding to Transport lines St Nicholas Camp G.1b.a.5.7. The Coy was training till 28-6-17.	
St Nicholas Camp to the line.	29-6-17		The Coy relieved the 50 M.G. Coy in the line on night of 29th/30th 8 guns in front & support line – 8 guns in reserve & barrage positions. gun positions as follows. 3 guns in Charlie Trench I.4.b.4.4. I.4.b.4.5. I.7.b.4.4. I.7.b.4.5. 2 South Comp Tr. I.1.c.9.15 & I.1.c.8.5.20. 3 in Coy Trench. I.1.c.4.4. I.1.a.60.25 I.1.a.50.45. One in Chili Tr. H.6.c.8.1. 2 in Hawthorn Tr. H.6.c.5.6. One in Helford Tr. H.6.a.3.0. & in Holly Tr. H.12.a.0.8. Ref Map for above BP 51.b.N.W. Trench map.	
In line.	30-6-17		Relief complete by 2 a.m.	

Signed M.Gilmour
Capt.

51st Machine Gun Coy.

51 M G Coy
Vol /8

Army Form C. 2118.

WAR DIARY
or
INTELLIGENCE SUMMARY.
(Erase heading not required.)

Instructions regarding War Diaries and Intelligence Summaries are contained in F.S. Regs., Part II. and the Staff Manual respectively. Title pages will be prepared in manuscript.

COMPANY HEADQUARTERS MAP REFERENCE BINCHE 1/20000 H5D80

Place	Date	Hour	Summary of Events and Information	Remarks and references to Appendices
	1/9/17		New anti-aircraft position made in HAZARD TRENCH just off CLYDE TRENCH. Indirect fire positions commenced in CHILI TRENCH about N6a8.2. Indirect fire:- 3000 rounds fired on the following targets:- Junction of road with MIDDLE TRENCH at I2a7370 - I8a6596 to I8b06. Junction of MIDDLE TRENCH with FARM at I2a58 MIDDLE TRENCH and I8a6695 to I8b06. Lieut. HAUGH returned from leave.	
	2/9/17		Indirect fire position in CHILI continued - Gun in CHILI H6 E 8.1 moved to H6 6 9.1 owing to bad field of fire. Anti-Aircraft - 350 Rounds fired during enemy at enemy planes. Indirect Fire - was carried out from 10.30pm - 12 midnight by guns in KOZY and HAWTHORNE TRENCHES on their junction at I3a3025 and GREENLAND HILL between I8b35 and I8b82.	
	3/9/17		At 10.15 am CORK TRENCH heavily shelled, one gun team 1/to 15 being killed:- 3636 Sgt AMBROSE W.E. 49949. Pte KINDZE H. 90036 Pte DORTON M. 71739 Pte OSBORNE N. 57352 - MOGG. S.H.E.	

T2134. Wt. W708-776. 500000. 4/15. Str J. C. & S.

Army Form C. 2118.

51st MACHINE GUN COMPANY

Instructions regarding War Diaries and Intelligence Summaries are contained in F. S. Regs., Part II. and the Staff Manual respectively. Title pages will be prepared in manuscript.

WAR DIARY
or
INTELLIGENCE SUMMARY.
(Erase heading not required.)

COMPANY HEADQUARTERS MAP REFERENCE BLACHE 1/20000 HS O 8.c.

Place	Date	Hour	Summary of Events and Information	Remarks and references to Appendices
	3/1/17		Indirect fire carried out by guns in HAWTHORNE TRENCH between 1.30 a.m. on WIDDLE TRENCH and I.8.a.65.95 to I.8.b.o.o. from 11 p.m. to midnight indirect fire was carried out by guns in HAWTHORNE and HOLLY TRENCHES on junction of MIDDLE TRENCH with track at I.2.a.5.8. - Track running from NEAR TRENCH at I.3.b.8.4. Track junction at I.3.a.30.25. WORK DONE – Indirect fire positions in CHILI carried on. Trenches to position dug & partly revetted. Gun damaged in CORK TRENCH withdrawn to repair. Night firing emplacement made in HAWTHORNE TRENCH – Two indirect fire positions started off CALEDONIAN TRENCH about H.6.6 d.5.75. Indirect fire – 2000 rounds fired from midnight 3rd/4th upon GREEN LAND HILL.	
	4/7/17		Lewis gun in CHARLIE TRENCH moved to "E" strong point in CHILI TRENCH. I.7.b.1.5.	

Army Form C. 2118.

WAR DIARY
or
INTELLIGENCE SUMMARY.
(Erase heading not required.)

57th MACHINE GUN COMPANY

Instructions regarding War Diaries and Intelligence Summaries are contained in F. S. Regs., Part II. and the Staff Manual respectively. Title pages will be prepared in manuscript.

Place	Date	Hour	Summary of Events and Information	Remarks and references to Appendices
	5/7/17		M.G.6 Emplacement in CHARLIE TRENCH altered to allow this gun to Coop COD TRENCH. Alternative emplacement to M.G.7. in CHARLIE completed.	
	6/7/17		2/Lt F.M. PASTEUR proceeds to 117 M.G. Company to take command. No. 14 Gun moved to T Sap E of COOK in CALEDONIAN - emplacement for two guns made. Shelters for teams in CUBA and COOK commenced. Work carried on with dug outs for positions N of CHILI and S of CALEDONIAN a depth of 10 feet has now been reached. 2/Lt JONATHAN proceeds on leave. R.E. completed shaft in CUBA strong point. Indirect Fire - 1000 rounds fired on WIT TRENCH I.I.B. - Two guns in CHARLIE and one gun in CUBA under Lt RICHARDSON relieved by three Gun Teams under 2/Lt MORRIS.	
	7/7/17		Upon relief three guns from CHARLIE and CUBA took up two positions in HOLLY and one in HAWTHORNE TRENCHES. 2/Lt ARNOLD returned from leave and joined the company in the line. Remainder 2/Lt HIGGINS relieved teams under 2/Lt KNAPP in COOK and CALEDONIAN TRENCH	

Company Headquarters Map Reference H6 B. 3.0.
BIACHE 10000

T2134. Wt. W708—776. 500000. 4/15. Sir J. C. & S.

War Diary / Intelligence Summary

Army Form C. 2118.

102nd MACHINE GUN COMPANY

Company Headquarters Map Reference: BIACHE H5.B.3.0. 1/20,000

Place	Date	Hour	Summary of Events and Information	Remarks and references to Appendices
	8/9/17		Three Guns placed in position in front of CHATZ TRENCH numbered 23-24-25. Indirect fire in cooperation with artillery was carried out by 4 guns Nos 23- 28- 29- 30 these guns fired as follows:- No. 29 from its own position - No. 28 from HAWTHORNE TRENCH No. 28 from CHILI TRENCH - No. 30 from CALEDONIAN TRENCH Number of rounds fired 750.- Enemy retaliation nil except on the guns in CALEDONIAN - on completion of firing all guns took up their S.O.S. positions again. Captain Gardner admitted to hospital - Lt. Haigh assumed Command of the Company.	
	9/9/17		Indirect fire carried out in cooperation with artillery on area between I.14.d.0.0. - I.20.6.0. I.20.d.0.8. - I.9.c.0.0. Guns No. 23- 28- 29. & 30 fired. 11.35 p.m. - 11.37 p.m. 12.20 a.m. - 12.22 a.m. 10/9/17. 2000 rounds - line of fire finished. Emplacements for Nos 23 and 27 guns finished - Alternative emplacements for Nos 12 & 13 guns commenced and trestles sandbagged.	
	10/9/17		Three guns No. 24. 25. 26. in front of CHATZ TRENCH under 2Lt Fripp relieved by three teams of No.1 section under 2Lt Nott - Upon relief the three	

51st MACHINE GUN COMPANY

WAR DIARY or INTELLIGENCE SUMMARY

Army Form C. 2118.

Place	Date	Hour	Summary of Events and Information	Remarks and references to Appendices
Company Headquarters - Map Reference BIRCHE 26cm H.5 & 6.0	10/4/17		Guns under 2/Lt Tripp took up positions vacated by No 1 Section as follows:- 1 team to HELFORD TRENCH MG. 30. 2 teams to HOLY TRENCH No. 23 & 28. No 87 position was occupied by team made up at Headquarters under Sgt Clarke.	
	11/4/17		Emplacements in HOLY and HAWTHORNE TRENCHES enlarged to suit position for use of elevating and traversing safety frames and shoes for tripod legs. Safety frame shoes fitted into place. Alternative emplacements commenced in CUBA & CHARLIE TRENCHES.	
	12/4/17		Heavy enemy shelling on CHARLIE and CUBA during night 11/12. No 8 and 15 Gun positions shelled.- No 14 Gun position in CALEDONIAN TRENCH wrecked.- Guns No. 28 & 30 moved from HOLY TRENCH H 12 a 0,8 to HAWTHORNE H 6 & 6.6. Tripod feet stops and elevating safety frame fittings, emplacements altered to suit. Rise guns were moved in order to conform with Divisional Defence & Barrage Scheme. - Anti-Aircraft- 350 Rounds fired at six enemy planes about 7.30 p.m. Planes driven off.	

T2134. Wt. W708—776. 500000. 4/15. Sir J. C. & S.

51st MACHINE GUN COMPANY.

Instructions regarding War Diaries and Intelligence Summaries are contained in F.S. Regs., Part II. and the Staff Manual respectively. Title pages will be prepared in manuscript.

WAR DIARY
or
INTELLIGENCE SUMMARY.
(Erase heading not required.)

Army Form C. 2118.

Place	Date	Hour	Summary of Events and Information	Remarks and references to Appendices
Germany HEADQUARTERS - NR FLERENGE Blache 20 ave. N9 8.8.0.	10/11/17		Enemy had two direct hits on Trenches occupied by Gun Teams, We had the following Casualties:- No 8 Gun in CORK TRENCH. Killed 81046 Pte MATHIAS. Died of Wounds 31506 Pte B. HUNT. Two men sent up from Headquarters to replace these Casualties. No 14 Gun in CALEDONIAN TRENCH moved into COZIN TRENCH I.D.5.5. to fire on enemy working parties in H.T TRENCH. Part of front line in COZIN and CONRAD cleared to enable this gun to fire - number of rounds fired 2000 - This gun was never tracked its original position before dawn. Guns numbered 27, 28, 29, & 30, in HAWTHORNE and HELLFORD TRENCHES fired in Cooperation with artillery on area enclosed by I8 a 44 - I8 d 5.5, I8 d 5.6. and I.F.C.9.6. Special attention being paid to road in I8 b. and E end of HART TRENCH in I8 d. No. of rounds fired 2500 - Swiss Rate of fire - 11.15 pm - 11.17 pm rapid fire - 11.17 pm -. 11.30 pm. burst of 50 rounds at irregular intervals.	

8th MACHINE GUN COMPANY

WAR DIARY or INTELLIGENCE SUMMARY

Army Form C. 2118.

Company Headquarters – Map Reference BIRCHE Seven N5 B 80.

Place	Date	Hour	Summary of Events and Information	Remarks and references to Appendices
	14/1/17		At 3.50 a.m. stray enemy shell landed in CHARLIE TRENCH and we had the following Casualties:- KILLED 58769 Pte N.N WATSON WOUNDED 53039 Sgt H. JOHNSON " 3607 Pte H.J. ROAT " 82334 - A. HINES An enemy Shell also landed in CALEDONIAN TRENCH at No 14 Gun position we had the following Casualties:- KILLED 57214 L/Cpl P. DYER " 72147 Pte G.E BENNETT * Wounded 89510 Pte T. URSELL Sergeant Young & three men from transport set up to replace Casualties. On the night of the 14th the 7th BORDER REGt carried out a raid from CONRAD TRENCH I.1.B upon WIT TRENCH fifty yards East & West of the C.T. at I.1.d.7.7. and C.T from I.1.b.7.7 to Trench Junction inclusive at I.1.b.65.85. Three guns in HAWTHORNE and one Gun in HELLFORD TRENCH fired on WIBBLE, WOBBLE and CROSS ROADS running E & S.E of WIND CROSS ROADS I.2.C.4.5. No of rounds fires 6000. Twice of firing	

51st Machine Gun Company

WAR DIARY or **INTELLIGENCE SUMMARY**

Army Form C. 2118.

Company Headquarters - Map Reference N.19.c.2.6.
Birche 2000

Place	Date	Hour	Summary of Events and Information	Remarks and references to Appendices
	14/7/17	10 - 10.30 pm	No 52 M.G. Bty sent up 16 men to go to each gun position to learn ground by daylight.	
	15/7/17		No 52 M.G. Coy sent up remainder of gun teams during afternoon, relief complete by 11.55pm. This company returned to St Nicholas Camp. G.17.C.5.7. Map 51 N.N.	
	16/7/17 to 23/7/17		Company remained in St Nicholas Camp. Requipped and training carried on.	
	22/7/17		One man from each gun team sent up line at 8pm. preceding 24 hours before rest of Company to obtain a knowledge of the routine.	
	23/7/17		The Company relieved the 50th Machine Gun Coy in the line on night of 23rd/24th. Gun positions as follows:- No 1 "Colombo" I.14.A.20.55. No 4 "Cupid" I.14.C.10.58. No 2 "Corona" I.14.C.05.90. No 3 "Cupid" I.14.A.00.95. No 5 "Curly" I.7.D.73.43. No 9 "Corona" Support I.13.B.53.25. No 10 "Coronna" Support I.13.B.40.90.	

51st MACHINE GUN COMPANY

Army Form C. 2118.

WAR DIARY or INTELLIGENCE SUMMARY.

(Erase heading not required.)

Place	Date	Hour	Summary of Events and Information	Remarks and references to Appendices
	23/9/17		A "A" Gun I.19.D. 95.49 Support guns	
			Barrage Guns	
			17 "Cordite" I.19.A. 3090	
			18 " — I.13.C. 1040	
			19 "Cawdor" Z.13.C. 2068	
			20 " — I.13.a. 2520	
			21 "Cadiz" H.12.D. 9535	
			22 " — H.12.d. 9545	
			31 "Camel" H.18.a. 9953	
			32 "Copper" H.18.a. 9060	
			Reference Map 1/10 above Plouvain 1/10000.	
	24/9/17	2.45 a.m.	Relief complete. Gun No.31 fired 50 rounds at A.A. emplacement in H.18.a 3535. SOS fired 50 rounds at aeroplane. Gun Nos. 21, 22, 31, & 32. H.12.D. 9535, H.12.D. 9545, H.16.a 9955 and H.18.a. 9080, respectively fired fire at 10.57 p.m. + 10 seconds. Artillery opened at 10.59 p.m. Rockets were fired at 10.59 p.m.	

T1134. Wt. W708-776. 500000. 4/15. Sir J. C. & S.

51st MACHINE GUN COMPANY

Army Form C. 2118.

WAR DIARY or INTELLIGENCE SUMMARY.
(Erase heading not required.)

Place	Date	Hour	Summary of Events and Information	Remarks and references to Appendices
	25/7/17		At 12 m.n. sentries were unable to pick up any blue rockets. Rockets were fired again at 2.10 p.m. All M.G's opened fire at 2.10 + 10 seconds. Artillery at 12.12 a.m. Sentries reported that the blue rockets were very hard to distinguish from our "Very lights". No 17.18.19.9.20 guns in I.19.a.30.90. I.13.c.10.90. I.13.c.20.68 & I.13.a.05.20. did not fire as no rockets were seen at all by sentries. Work done. New emplacement started for No 9 Gun in I.13.b.5325. Position of No 3 Gun found to be T.14.c.a5.60. No 3 gun was moved about 30 yds to left away from junction of "CHEMICAL" C.T. to present position was being in a 15/53. The alterations in the positions of No 3 & 9 guns were ordered by C.S.O. Division. During night of 25/26 guns No 17+18. I.19.a.30.90. & I 13.c.10.40. fired 2,520 rounds on tracks at I.9.C.65.35. All trenches improved and strengthened with sandbags. No 31 Gun from its A.A. position in H.18.a.35.55" fired 250 rounds at enemy 'plane.	
	26/7/17		On night of 26th in co-operation with Artillery we fired as follows.	

Company Hdqtrs – M.G Reserve
Biettie Depot   H.19.c.2.6.

WAR DIARY or INTELLIGENCE SUMMARY

Army Form C. 2118.

51st Coy. Machine Gun Corps

Place	Date	Hour	Summary of Events and Information	Remarks and references to Appendices
			Gun No 17 at I.19.a.3595 and Gun No.18 at I.13.C.1535 fired 3,000 rounds on junction of Railway and road at I.9.C.6535. Gun No.19 at I.13.C.0570 fired 1,000 rounds on road at I.15.B.00.65 and Gun No 20 fired 1500 rounds on road at I.15.B.10.10. Time ZERO & ZERO + 6. ZERO + 14 & ZERO + 20, sinking bursts of fire after that ZERO 10.50pm bursts of 50 rounds every 20 minutes throughout the night. Gun No 21 at H.12.d.7530 & gun No 22 at H.12.d.7545 fired 2,000 rounds at I.9.a.9595. Same rate and rate of fire same as above. Anti-aircraft. 200 rounds fired from A.A. position in "CRETE". H.24.d.8585. Enemy plane driven off. Gun No 9 moved from I.13.B.5325 to new position at I.13.B.5520 to enable it to have a better field of fire. All trenches and emplacements cleared deepened, & strengthened with extra sandbags. 2/Lt Wright returned from Hospital and remains at Transport line for the present.	
	27/9/17		During the night the following was fired. Gun No 17 at I.19.a.3595 fired on I.15.B.8565. Gun No.18 at I.13.C.1535 fired on I.15.B.4565.	

WAR DIARY or INTELLIGENCE SUMMARY

51st Coy Machine Gun Corps

Army Form C. 2118.

Place	Date	Hour	Summary of Events and Information	Remarks and references to Appendices
Company H.Q. Blaihe 9200 Mag Rajeune H.19.B.2.6	28/29/17		Rounds fired by the two Guns 1750. Gun No 17 was firing along a road in PLOUVAIN whilst No 18 Gun fired at the junction of four roads leading into PLOUVAIN. From track map these seemed to be places of likely enemy activity. Gun No 21 at M.12.D.9530 fired on I.9.a.9505. " 22 " M.12.D.9505 " I.9.a.9505. Rounds fired by these two guns 2,000. This last map reference is shown on track map as a point where enemy tracks meet. Anti-aircraft gun at H.24.b.8555 fired 500 rounds at enemy planes. All of these within range driven off. Work done. New anti-aircraft position commenced at M.18.D.8590. A detachment of the 7th East Yorkshire Regt. (50th Inf Brigade) raided IN.12. and COST trenches on the night of July 28/29th with the object of securing identification, destroying enemy trench Mortars, Machine Guns and dug-outs in the railway Cutting between CORK, COST & CANDY trenches. Zero hour was 12.30 a.m July 28/29th. Eight of our machine-guns co-operated with the Artillery as follows:- Two guns Nos 31 and 32 were moved from their positions at H.18.a.8545.	

51st Company Machine Gun Corps

Army Form C. 2118.

WAR DIARY or INTELLIGENCE SUMMARY
(Erase heading not required.)

Place	Date	Hour	Summary of Events and Information	Remarks and references to Appendices
Coy Headquarters BIACHE 20,000 H.19.a.2.6			and H.18.a.95.95. respectively and placed between Guns No.17 & 18. in CORDITE Trench. The positions of the guns were :- No.17 I.19.a.35.95. No.19 I.19.a.35.95. = 31. I.13.c.26.05. No.16 A = 32 I.13.c.20.20. No.18 I.13.c.15.35. These four guns formed a standing barrage South of Railway between I.14.F.70.00 - I.14.b.55.35. I.14.B.90.45 - I.15.A.00.15. Guns No.19 at I.13.c.05.70. " 20 " H.18.B.95.15. " 21 " H.12.D.75.30 " 22 " H.12.D.70.45 formed a standing barrage North of Railway between I.6.D.50.85 - I.8.C.60.00 - I.8.D.80.50 between ZERO and ZERO + 30 minutes. Rate of fire. 1 Belt per gun every 3 minutes. Total number of rounds fired by the right guns 19,500 rounds. Guns Nos 31 & 32 were taken back to their original positions, all guns again laid on their barrage lines. 2/Lt Wright found 2/Lt Amos to assist in Aviation remained with him. Section Officers report guns fired well, a few stoppages over No.3 r.H.	

Army Form C. 2118.

51st Coy Machine Gun Corps

WAR DIARY
or
INTELLIGENCE SUMMARY.
(Erase heading not required.)

Instructions regarding War Diaries and Intelligence Summaries are contained in F. S. Regs., Part II. and the Staff Manual respectively. Title pages will be prepared in manuscript.

Company Headquarters
BIRCHE 1000

H 19 c 2.6
Map Ref

Place	Date	Hour	Summary of Events and Information	Remarks and references to Appendices
	29/30th		The futures due to slack shells. Work of improving trenches was continued. Most of the time after firing being taken up in filling belts. Between the hours of midnight and 3am 29th/30th the following guns fired a road running through I.15.c and upon the bank in I.15.c+d. From maps it is observed that these localities are much used by the enemy as tracks leading to their trenches. Information has been received that an enemy relief is to take place during the above hours. The guns fired as follows:	
			No 9 Gun on I 19 a 3595 on I 13 c 4055	
			" 18 " " I 13 c 1535 " I 15 c 6095	
			" 19 " " I 13 c 0590 " I 15 c 6590	
			" 20 " " H 18 b 9515 " I 15 c 9565	
			" 21 " " H 12 D 7530 " I 15 c 0525	
			" 22 " " H 12 D 7845 " I 15 c 2540	
			" 31 " " H 18 A 5545 " I 15 c 2510	
			" 32 " " H 18 A 7595 " I 14 D 9010	
				Total rounds fired 6,500

Army Form C. 2118.

51st Coy. Machine Gun Corps.

WAR DIARY
or
INTELLIGENCE SUMMARY.
(Erase heading not required.)

Place	Date	Hour	Summary of Events and Information	Remarks and references to Appendices
Bompany Fabe Biache / Yser	30/9/17		New position started for No 5 Gun at I.7.D.6530 — Shafts of New sap at I.14.a.00,95 finished and chamber commenced. Heavy showers during the day prevented much work being done on trenches. Enemy artillery had been comparatively quiet up to to-day. At 11am up to 4.30 p.m. the enemy shelled the area between CHEMICAL, CUPID, CAMBRIAN T CUBA. In all about 200 shells, mostly 5.9 or heavier fell in this area. CUPID was blown in at junction with COCK — junction of CAMBRIAN — CUPID was completely filled in. No 5 Gun position in CUPID was blown in Tripod and belt box on the emplacement were blown on to the parados. Damage done, to as set of ammunition exploded and one boot missing. Probably buried. Indirect fire during night 30/9/31st. Gun No. 21. H.12.D.7630. " 22. H.12.D.9545 } fired on I.9.a.9505. This point is shewn on 62 Map* " a Track Junction. Gun No.31 H.18.a.15,45 Gun No.32. H.18.a.95,75 fired on I.15.a.30,65 a junction	

Army Form C. 2118.

51st Coy Machine Gun Company WAR DIARY or INTELLIGENCE SUMMARY.

Instructions regarding War Diaries and Intelligence Summaries are contained in F.S. Regs., Part II. and the Staff Manual respectively. Title pages will be prepared in manuscript.

(Erase heading not required.)

Place	Date	Hour	Summary of Events and Information	Remarks and references to Appendices
	31/7/17		A road leading from PLOUVAIN and track running to enemy's front line through I.14. Central.	
			Total rounds fired by the above 4 guns 2,500.	
			All men of 236 M.G. Coy who were with our teams in the line returned to ROCLINCOURT VALLEY camp at 4.0am 31st	These men, 32 in all, were in the line with no instruction
			Indirect fire was carried out during the night as follows.	
			Gun No 21 H.12.D.9530)	
			" 22 H.12.D.75'45) on I.9.a.9505. Junction of four tracks.	
			" 31 H.18.A.1545)	
			" 32 H.18.A.9575) to I.15.a.3065. Junction of PLOUVAIN road and track running to enemy's front line through I.14. Central. Total rounds fired by the four guns 2,500	
			Four Guns of 236th Machine Gun Coy relieved our four guns No 17,18, 19 + 20. Relief complete by 11 P.m. Our four guns came back into FAMPOUX into Brigade Reserve.	
			2/Lt Arnold and 2/Lt Wright came back to Company Headquarters.	

Company Headquarters
BIACHE 2000
H.19.2.6.

Army Form C. 2118.

51st Coy Machine Gun Corps

WAR DIARY
or
INTELLIGENCE SUMMARY.
(Erase heading not required.)

Instructions regarding War Diaries and Intelligence Summaries are contained in F. S. Regs., Part II. and the Staff Manual respectively. Title pages will be prepared in manuscript.

Place	Date	Hour	Summary of Events and Information	Remarks and references to Appendices
			The four guns of 236th Machine Gun Coy come under the direct orders of O.C. 51st Machine Gun Coy. Weather which up to three days ago, had been very fine has broken down & considerably hampered work in the Trenches.	
			D. Stacey Hayes R. Lieut. Commanding 51st Coy M.G. Corps.	

51st Coy Machine Gun Corps

WAR DIARY
or
INTELLIGENCE SUMMARY
(Erase heading not required.)

Army Form C. 2118.

Vol 19

Place	Date	Hour	Summary of Events and Information	Remarks and references to Appendices
In the field	1/8/1917		Effective Strength of Company on this date 10 Officers 191 Other Ranks. Indirect fire was carried out during the night as follows:—	
"	2nd		No 17 Gun at I.19.a.3595 fired on I.15.B.8565	
			" 18 " " I.13.C.1035 " " I.15.B.8565	
			" 19 " " I.13.C.0590 " " I.15.B.4560	
			" 20 " " H.18.B.9515 " " I.15.B.4560	
			Nos 17 & 18 Guns were firing along the main street in PROUVIN Nos 19 & 20 guns on Junction of four cross roads just outside PROUVIN.	
			No 21 gun at H.12.D.9530 fired on I.15.B.0565 } These two guns were searching roads	
			" 22 " " H.12.D.9545 " " I.15.B.2088 } leading out of PROUVIN.	
			Gun No 31 at H.13.a.8545 " " I.9.C.6535 — Junction of four cross roads.	
			" " 32 " H.18.a.7595 " " I.9.C.3014 — Enfilading CLAY Trench.	
			Total number of rounds fired 7,500.	
			During the day we carried out instructional reliefs as follows. No. 4 Section under 2/Lt Wright relieved No. 3 Section under 2/Lt F.M. Higgins. and took over the following guns. No 1, 2, 9 & 10.	

Coy. H.Q. H.17.c.9.6.

Army Form C. 2118.

51st Coy Machine Gun Corps.

WAR DIARY
or
INTELLIGENCE SUMMARY.
(Erase heading not required.)

Instructions regarding War Diaries and Intelligence Summaries are contained in F. S. Regs., Part II. and the Staff Manual respectively. Title pages will be prepared in manuscript.

Place	Date	Hour	Summary of Events and Information	Remarks and references to Appendices
In the field			No 3 Section relieved No 2 Section under 2/Lt A.C Noble and took over Nos 3, 4, 5, 11 guns	
			No 2 Section relieved No 1 Section under 2/Lt T McTripp and took over Nos 20, 21, 31 & 32 guns	
			N. 2 & 6 M.G.Coy being in charge of 17, 18, 19, & 20 guns.	
			No 1 Section came back into Brigade Reserve FAMPOUX dug-outs at H.23.a.4.9. Weather still continues bad, raining more or less all the time.	
	27/3rd		Indirect fire was carried out during the night by Guns No 17, 18, 19, 20, 21, 22, 31 & 32 on same targets as 1st/2nd. Total rounds fired 9,700. Harried all day. Unable to do much work in trenches.	
	3rd/4		During the night in co-operation with the Artillery indirect fire was carried out as under. Nos 17 & 18 Guns at I.19.a.3595 and I.13.c.1635 searched road running through I.15.c & 13. No 19 & 20 Guns at I.13.c.0570 and H.6.D.9515 searched track running through I.8.D.9030 to I.9 Central. No 21 & 22 guns at H.12.d.9530 and H.12.D.7545 searched track running from I.8.B.8505 through	

51st Coy Machine Gun Corps.

Army Form C. 2118.

WAR DIARY
or
INTELLIGENCE SUMMARY.
(Erase heading not required.)

Instructions regarding War Diaries and Intelligence Summaries are contained in F. S. Regs., Part II. and the Staff Manual respectively. Title pages will be prepared in manuscript.

Place	Date	Hour	Summary of Events and Information	Remarks and references to Appendices
In the field.			T. & Co B. No 31 & 32 guns at H.18.a.35/45. and H.18.a.75/75. reached road running from I.15.a.30.65 into PROUVAIN. Number of rounds fired 10,100. Rate of fire. Bursts of 50 rounds every 20 minutes during the night. Rapid fire for one minute at 10-35 p.m. & 10-45 a.m. 236. No. 9 Coy. at 17, 18, 19 & 20 guns. 2/Lt. Dann relieved 2/Lt. Allen.	
	4/5.		Guns 17, 18, 19, 20, 21, 22, 31, & 32 fired 7,000 rounds on same targets as on night 3/4. Firing was in bursts of 50 rounds every 20 minutes throughout the night. There was no rapid fire for one minute at 10.35 p.m. & 10-45 p.m. 2/Lt. O.A. Grantham returned from leave to U.K. on 4/5/1917 and remained at Transport Lines.	
	5/6.		On the night of 5th inst the 10th Sherwood Foresters sent out three patrols consisting of 1 Officer & 10 men each, to get into CRUST, COAL, & CUB lines of shell holes, on the lines approximately I.14.c.80.62 to I.14.c.70.94 in order to get an identification and any prisoners and M.G's which they may find. The action of machine guns was to search various areas which was done as follows. 4 Guns in CORDITE Norp at I.19.a.35.95 searched tracks leading from the ROEUX – "I7a." I.13.c.26.05 SPROUVAIN road to CYPRUS trench I.13.c – I.14.D.	

T2184. Wt. W708–776. 500000. 4/15. Sir J. C. & S.

Army Form C. 2118.

51st Coy Machine Gun Corps

WAR DIARY
or
INTELLIGENCE SUMMARY.
(Erase heading not required.)

Instructions regarding War Diaries and Intelligence Summaries are contained in F. S. Regs., Part II. and the Staff Manual respectively. Title pages will be prepared in manuscript.

Place	Date	Hour	Summary of Events and Information	Remarks and references to Appendices
In the field			No 18 gun at I.13.c.1535 ⎫ searched french system of CYRIL, CLIFF, CHIN and	
			" 18A " " I.13.c.2020 ⎬ CUB. I.13.d.	
			Four guns in CAWDOR Trench.	
			No 19 gun at I.13.c.0590 ⎫	
			" 19A " " I.13.c.0585 ⎬ searched DELBAR WOOD. I.21.a.	
			" 20 " " H.13.b.9515 ⎬	
			" 20A " " I.13.a.0500 ⎭ searched HAUSA WOOD I.21.a.	
			Four guns in CADIZ and COPPER	
			No 21 gun at H.12.D.9530 ⎫ searched tracks leading from WET to WART trench I.8.B.	
			" 22 " " H.12.D.9545 ⎬ I.9.a.	
			No 30 " " H.18.a.8545 ⎬ searched tracks leading from WORM to WART trench	
			" 33 " " H.18.a.9575 ⎭ I.18.D. — I.9.c.	
			Time + Rate of fire.	
			Intense from Z to Z + 14 minutes. From Z + 14 onwards till dawn bursts of 50 rounds every 20 minutes. The four guns in Brigade Reserve were moved up and took up position Two in CORDITE Nos 19 + 18A. Two in CANDOR Nos 19 + 20A. Map Reference as above.	

Army Form C. 2118.

51st Coy Machine Gun Corps

WAR DIARY
or
INTELLIGENCE SUMMARY.

(Erase heading not required.)

Instructions regarding War Diaries and Intelligence Summaries are contained in F. S. Regs., Part II. and the Staff Manual respectively. Title pages will be prepared in manuscript.

Place	Date	Hour	Summary of Events and Information	Remarks and references to Appendices
In the field	6/7/17		The four guns were withdrawn at 2.t.20. and taken back to dug-outs in FAMPOUX and came into Brigade Reserve. Total number of rounds fired 21,600. Indirect fire was carried out during the night by the same guns and on the same targets as on night of 1/2nd instant. Total number of rounds fired 7,000.	
	7/7		P. McKirry and four teams of 236th M.G. Coy. relieved 2/Lt Rowe and four teams of same Company. Geo No. 17, 18, 19, 8, 20. at 10.30 p.m. on the night of 6/7. New emplacements started in Isbernsheole line as follows:- H.19.B.25.20. H.19.B.30.40. H.11.c.86.65. H.11.c.90.60. Reference map BIACHE. 1:20,000. During the night indirect fire was carried out by the same guns and on the same targets as on night of 6/7/17 inst. These targets were trenches and roads leading from PLOUVAIN Geos 20.21 & 22 were unable to fire during the early part of the night owing to working parties in front of CpDlz. At 3.50 a.m. S.O.S. signal went up and guns were laid on their barrage line and fire opened. The enemy under cover of Artillery fire raided our front line trenches COPR. T. CUCKBURN, but were driven out. They obtained no prisoners, but left some of their dead and wounded in our trenches.	

T2134. Wt. W708-776. 500000. 4/15. Sir J. C. & S.

51st Coy Machine Gun Corps

Army Form C. 2118.

WAR DIARY
or
INTELLIGENCE SUMMARY.
(Erase heading not required.)

Instructions regarding War Diaries and Intelligence Summaries are contained in F. S. Regs., Part II. and the Staff Manual respectively. Title pages will be prepared in manuscript.

Place	Date	Hour	Summary of Events and Information	Remarks and references to Appendices
In the field			Two guns No 3 and 5 in CUPID opened fire in addition to the Barrage guns. Situation quietened down at 4.45 a.m. From information received from one of the prisoners taken by the Infantry it transpires that the troops employed on the raid were special Storm troops brought up the night before. We had two casualties N 13526 Pte Tippet T.N. and N 68359 Pte Longford. M. Both wounded by shell-fire. During the afternoon of the 8th the Company was relieved by 52nd M.G. Coy. Relief commenced at 2.30 p.m was completed at 7.50 p.m. The Company marched back to GRIMSBY CAMP. Map Ref. 51 B.N.W. G.19.a.10.20. The tour in the trenches was a quiet one with the exception of the raid. The enemy was active with Trench Mortars and Machine Guns. During the nights the enemy consistently shelled the CHEMICAL WORKS. Our air craft were strenuously against our air craft. Lieut A Duncan joined the Company as reinforcement from the 17th Div Depot Battalion. 2/Lieut J D Mann rejoins from Hospital.	Pte Tippett died of wounds on 12.8.17
	9/8		Company carried on with training and re-equipping. On night of 15th one gun team was sent up the line to become	

51st Coy Machine Gun Corps.

Army Form C. 2118.

WAR DIARY
or
INTELLIGENCE SUMMARY

Place	Date	Hour	Summary of Events and Information	Remarks and references to Appendices
In the field	16th		Families with positions held by 50th M.G. Coy in left sector. 2/Lt A.C. Noble proceeded on leave to U.K. on 9th inst. 2/Lt. 6 Wright on 13/8/17. Company relieved 50: M.G. Coy in the line. Relief commenced at 3p.m. complete by 7.30 p.m. Headquarters in HUSSAR Trench and gun positions as follows:— Reference BOUVAIN map 1/10.000.	
			Gun No 6. I.7.B. 40.35. Gun No 6a. I.7.B.3590. Gun No 9. I.7.B. 3595.	
			" 12. I.7.B. 00.45 " 13. I.7.a. 9065. " 14. I.1.c. 9550.	
			" 8. I.1.c. 95.65 " 15. I.1.a. 6515. " 16. I.1.a. 5540.	
			" 23. H.12.B. 75.45 " 23a. H.12.B. 6590 " 24. H.6.D. 4505.	
			" 24a. H.6.D. 55.95 " 25. H.6.D. 6095. " 26. H.6.B. 4530.	
			" 27. H.6.a. 3505 " 28. H.6.c. 5070.	
			and three guns in Intermediate line the positions of which had not been definitely located.	
			Guns No. 24 & 28 fired from 10-30 p.m. throughout the night upon roads and tracks leading to RAILWAY COPSE.— The targets were No.24 gun on L.2.B. 9525. Gun No 28 on I.3.a. 3025. Number of rounds fired 2.800.	
	17/8/17			

WAR DIARY or INTELLIGENCE SUMMARY

Army Form C. 2118.

51st Coy. Machine Gun Corps

Place	Date	Hour	Summary of Events and Information	Remarks and references to Appendices
In the field	17/18th		Indirect fire was carried out throughout the night by the following guns.	
			No 23ª gun engaged targets on I.8.B.3050	
			" 24 " " " " " I.3.C.5000	
			" 27 " " " " " I.2.d.3050	
			" 28 " " " " " SQUARE WOOD.	
			The first three references are Trench Mortar emplacements & tracks.	
			Total number of rounds fired 5,000.	
			Captᵗ Simpson relieved 2/Lt. Sam taking over the four guns I.E.#, 27, 28, 25 & 26 belonging to 236ᵗ M.G. Company.	
	18/19		Indirect fire was carried out throughout the night by the following Guns No 23. on I.8.B.4540. Trench Mortar emplacement.	
			" 24 " " I.3.C.1030 Enemy trenches.	
			" 28 " " I.3.a.2525 Cross Roads.	
			" 27 " " C.27.c.01 SQUARE WOOD.	
			Total number of rounds fired 6,000.	
	19/20.		Throughout the night, indirect fire was carried on as follows:—	

Army Form C. 2118.

WAR DIARY
or
INTELLIGENCE SUMMARY.
(Erase heading not required.)

57th Coy Machine Gun Corps

Instructions regarding War Diaries and Intelligence Summaries are contained in F. S. Regs., Part II. and the Staff Manual respectively. Title pages will be prepared in manuscript.

Place	Date	Hour	Summary of Events and Information	Remarks and references to Appendices
In the field	19th/20th		Gun No 23 on I.8.B.4540. – Trench Mortar emplacements Tracks.	
			" 23a " I.8.B.3050 – " "	
			" 24 " I.8.C.5000 – " "	
			" 24a " I.3.C.1030 – Enemy Tracks.	
			" 27 " I.2.a.5000 – " "	
			" 28 " C.26.D.3015 – " "	
			From 3.45 – 4.30 pm gun No 24 fired on I.B.80.50 and dispersed enemy working parties. This was done with observation from front line. Rounds fired 580.	
			The map references of these guns on INTERMEDIATE LINE are.	
			No 9 gun #11.A.8099. No 10 gun H.5.C.9930. No 11 gun H.5.a.8925.	
	20/21st		Indirect fire as follows.	
			Gun No.23 on I.2.C.5060. – Road leading to WHIP CROSS roads.	
			" 23a " I.3.C.6020 – Enemy Tracks.	
			" 24 " I.8.D.5020 – Tracks at WINDMILL COPSE	
			" 24a " I.8.D.3020 – Machine Gun emplacement.	

Army Form C. 2118.

51st Coy Machine Gun Corps.

WAR DIARY
or
INTELLIGENCE SUMMARY.
(Erase heading not required.)

Instructions regarding War Diaries and Intelligence Summaries are contained in F.S. Regs., Part II. and the Staff Manual respectively. Title pages will be prepared in manuscript.

Place	Date	Hour	Summary of Events and Information	Remarks and references to Appendices
In the field	20th/21st		Gun No 24 on I.8.B.6540 — Enemy Dump.	
			" 28 " I.3.a.2550 — Track Junction.	
			Anti-aircraft position at No.12 fired 500 rounds at E.A. Total rounds fired 8,000. During the night 20th/21st No 236 M.G. Coy carried out an anti-aircraft fire of 25, 26, 24 & 28 guns.	
	21/22nd		Indirect fire was carried out as follows:—	
			Gun No 23 on L.8.B.4540 — Track & road junction.	
			" " 23a " I.8.B.3.5. — Trench Mortar emplacement	
			" " 24 " I.3.C.5.0. — " 8 Tracks	
			" " 24a " I.3.c.10.30. — Tracks.	
			" " 24 " I.3.a.3.3. — Cross Roads.	
			" " 28 " I.8.D.5.2 — Tracks at Windmill Copse.	
			Total rounds fired 7,000. A.A. position at No. 12 fired 250 rounds at	
			E.A. — driven off.	
	22/23rd		Indirect fire was carried out as follows. Gun No 23 on I.9.C.I.5 Tracks Morn Trench Gun No 23a on I.8.d.4525:— Tracks at Windmill Copse. Gun No 24 on I.4.B.4.9:— Railway Embkt.	

51st Coy Machine Gun Corps

Army Form C. 2118.

WAR DIARY
or
INTELLIGENCE SUMMARY.
(Erase heading not required.)

Instructions regarding War Diaries and Intelligence Summaries are contained in F. S. Regs., Part II. and the Staff Manual respectively. Title pages will be prepared in manuscript.

Place	Date	Hour	Summary of Events and Information	Remarks and references to Appendices
In the field	22/23		Gun No 24ª fired on I.8.d.25.50. – Tracks	
			" 27 " " I.8.B.4.4. Tracks & SUNKEN Road.	
			" 28 " " I.8.a.75.10 Tracks.	
			Total number of rounds fired 7,250	
	23rd/24		In co-operation with Artillery & Trench Mortars machine guns fired during the night as follows. Gun No 23, 23ª, 24, 24, 25, 26. Searched ground enclosed by I.8.0.7.5. I.9.Central. I.9.d.00. I.14.b.2.5.	
			Gun No 27. fired on I.6.b.4.4. – Enemy Trucks	
			" 28 " " I.8.a.75.10 – do –	
			Time & Rate of fire. From ZERO +1 to ZERO +8. – intense bursts of fire.	
			Thoughts throughout the night firing was kept up intermittently on the above targets.	
			Total number of rounds fired 15,000.	
	24th		Lieut. Duncan and 16.01 Section relieved 2/Lieut Mann and No 2 Section in CORK SUPPORT. 2/Lt. Mann & No 2 Section relieved Lieut. Duncan and No 1. Section in CHICKEN RESERVE. No 3 Section changed over with No 4 Section.	
			Lieut Fripp proceeded in CHARLIE TRENCH. 2/Lt. Arnold came back to H.Qtrs.	

Army Form C. 2118.

51st Divl Machine Gun Corps

WAR DIARY
or
INTELLIGENCE SUMMARY.
(Erase heading not required.)

Instructions regarding War Diaries and Intelligence Summaries are contained in F. S. Regs., Part II. and the Staff Manual respectively. Title pages will be prepared in manuscript.

Place	Date	Hour	Summary of Events and Information	Remarks and references to Appendices
In the field	24th/25th		Indirect fire was carried out throughout the night as below:—	
			Gun No 23 fired on T.9.c.0090. Tracks.	
			" " 24 " " C.27.c.0510 "	
			" " 23.A " " C.27.c.0510 "	
			" " 21A " " T.9.c.0090 "	
			" " 27 " " T.2.D.0520 WEED TRENCH	
			" " 28 " " T.8.D.0565 Tracks. Total number of rounds fired	
			8,570. 2/Lt Higgins relieves 2/Lt Mann.	
	25th/26th		Usual indirect fire carried out as follows.	
			Gun No 24 fired on T.9.a.45.10. Tracks.	
			" " 24.A " " T.9.a.4575 "	
			" " 25 " " T.2.D.9540 "	
			" " 26 " " T.2.D.9560 "	
			" " 27 " " T.8.a.9010 "	
			" " 28 " " T.8.B.0510. "	
			Total number of rounds fired 9,250	

Army Form C. 2118.

51st Coy. Machine Gun Corps

WAR DIARY
or
INTELLIGENCE SUMMARY.
(Erase heading not required.)

Instructions regarding War Diaries and Intelligence Summaries are contained in F.S. Regs., Part II. and the Staff Manual respectively. Title pages will be prepared in manuscript.

Place	Date	Hour	Summary of Events and Information	Remarks and references to Appendices
In the field	26th/27th		Indirect fire was carried out during the night as follows.	
			Gun No 24 Target I.9.a.4590 Description:- Tracks	
			" 24A " I.9.a.4595 " "	
			" 27 " I.2.D.0520 " WEED TRENCH.	
			" 28 " I.8.B.0570 " Tracks.	
			Total number of rounds 5,500.	
	27th		2/Lieut. C. Wright returns from leave on this date. 2/Lt Tipp changed places with 2/Lt Loggins. Lieut Jordan relieved Lieut Duncan in CORK SUPPORT. Lieut Duncan returned to Coy Hd Qrs and took over No 4 Section's guns in INTERMEDIATE LINE.	
	27th/28th:		Indirect fire was carried out during the night as follows.	
			Gun No 24 Target I.9.a.4590. Description:- Tracks	
			" 24A " I.9.a.4595. " "	
			" 27 " I.2.D.0520. " WEED TRENCH	
			" 28. " I.8.B.0570 " Tracks.	
			Number of rounds fired :- 5,000.	

Army Form C. 2118.

51st Coy. Machine Gun Corps

WAR DIARY
or
INTELLIGENCE SUMMARY.
(Erase heading not required.)

Place	Date	Hour	Summary of Events and Information	Remarks and references to Appendices
In the field	28/29		Indirect fire was carried out during the night as follows.	
			Gun No 24. Target I.9.a.6.6. TRACK WARD TRENCH	
			" 24 a. " I.8.c.6.1.? TRACK & BRICKWORK LANE.	
			" 25. " I.3.c.6.1.	
			" 26 " I.3.a.25.50 TRACKS	
			" 27. " I.8.B.4.4. —"—	
			" 28. " I.8.D.5.2. —"—	
			Total Number of rounds fired 8,500.	
	29/30		In Co-operation with the Artillery Indirect fire was carried out as under during the night:—	
			Gun No 23. fired on I.14.B.70.25. Time 2.0 a.m.	
			" " 23A " —"— " —"—	
			" " 23 " I.9. Central " 2.40 a.m.	
			" " 23 A " —"— " —"—	
			" " 23 " I.14.D.30.50 " 3.15 a.m.	
			" " 23 A " —"— " —"—	

51st Coy Machine Gun Corps

WAR DIARY
or
INTELLIGENCE SUMMARY.
(Erase heading not required.)

Army Form C. 2118.

Place	Date	Hour	Summary of Events and Information	Remarks and references to Appendices
In the field	29/30th		Gun No 24 fired on I.8.a.8010 at 2.5 am	
			" " 28 " " " " 2.45 am	
			" " 27 " I.3.a.2050 " "	
			" " 28 " " " "	
			" " 26 " I.14.B.4025 " 2.0 am	
			" " 25 " " " "	
			" " 24 " I.8.D.35.25 " 2.15 am	
			" " 24ᴬ " " " "	
			" " 25 " I.3.A.8500 " 3.5 am	
			" " 26 " " " "	
			" " 24ᵃ " " " "	
			Rate of fire Intense bursts for one minute. After 3.15 am guns fired intermittently until dawn on targets which each gun was last laid upon.	
			Total number of rounds 10,250.	
			In co-operation with Artillery indirect fire was carried out as follows:-	
	30th/31st			

Army Form C. 2118.

51st Coy Machine Gun Corps

WAR DIARY
or
INTELLIGENCE SUMMARY.
(Erase heading not required.)

Instructions regarding War Diaries and Intelligence Summaries are contained in F.S. Regs., Part II. and the Staff Manual respectively. Title pages will be prepared in manuscript.

Place	Date	Hour	Summary of Events and Information	Remarks and references to Appendices
In the field	30/8	3.0 pm	Gun No 23. ⎫ Target. I.15.c.1.3 to I.15 Central.	
			" " 28. ⎭	
			" " 25. ⎫ " Clod Trench between C.18 and Cliff.	
			" " 26. ⎭	
			" " 24. ⎫ " Road I.14.B.4067 to Plouvain.	
			" " 24. ⎭	
			" " 27. ⎫ " Railway Cutting from Windmill Copse.	
			" " 28. ⎭	
			Bursts of fire were first down at 10 p.m. 10.15 p.m. 2.30 a.m. 2.20 a.m. 2.45 a.m. and 2.50 a.m. thereafter intermittently throughout the night. Total number of rounds fired 10,500. 2/Lt. Noble returned from leave 30/8/17. During the morning of 31/8/1917. No. 103491. Pte Brown D.M. was wounded.	

D. Hosegood
Capt. Comm. O/ing 51 M.G. Coy

31-8-17

Army Form C. 2118.

51st Company Machine Gun Corps

WAR DIARY
or
INTELLIGENCE SUMMARY.
(Erase heading not required.)

September 1st 1917   Vol 20

Place	Date	Hour	Summary of Events and Information	Remarks and references to Appendices
In the field	Aug 31st/ Sept 1st		Effective Strength of Unit on this date :— Officers 11. O.R's 168. Indirect fire was carried out during the night as follows Gun No 25 Target I.9 Central.	
			" " 23ᵃ } " Iguan Wood.	
			" " 24ᵃ }	
			" " 24 " T.3.c.10.30. Tracks.	
			" " 25 " T.3.c.6.1. "	
			" " 26 " T.3.a.25.50. "	
			" " 27 " I.8.d.35.20. "	
			" " 28 " I.8.d.5.2. "	
			Total number of rounds fired. — 7.500. On the night of 31st/1st No 52 Machine Gun Company sent up one man to each position in order to become familiar with the ground. During the afternoon of 1st Sep the remainder of 52nd M.G.Coy came up. Relief commenced at 3 o'clock and was complete by 6-25 pm. The 51st M.G.Coy returned to GRIMSBY CAMP. REF.MAP. 57B NW. Map 24. G.17.a.1.2.	

Army Form C. 2118.

21st Company Machine Gun Corps

WAR DIARY
or
INTELLIGENCE SUMMARY.
(Erase heading not required.)

Instructions regarding War Diaries and Intelligence Summaries are contained in F. S. Regs., Part II. and the Staff Manual respectively. Title pages will be prepared in manuscript.

Place	Date	Hour	Summary of Events and Information	Remarks and references to Appendices
In the field			The tour in the line was a quiet one. There was comparatively little shelling by the enemy who seemed to be relying upon his Trench Mortars even more than during our previous tour in this sector. Enemy M.G's were very active during the day against our aeroplanes. The weather was good. Although we did have one or two very wet days, but owing to the good work in the way of draining and duckboarding the trenches did not suffer to any great extent. During this tour we experimented with "Pit-Prop" mountings, designed by the 77th Company R.E., for indirect fire at night, keeping our tripod mounting in the battle emplacement. These mountings proved very satisfactory, so in addition to being steady and it being impossible for the mounting to sink, they are practically invisible to enemy aeroplanes.	
	1st Sep.		Lt. A.R. Fraser proceeds on leave to U.K.	
	1/5		Remained at Camp, reequipping and training.	
	5th Sep.		The Company sent up one man per Team to go to each gun position occupied by the 50th M.G. Coy. in the CHEMICAL WORKS sector in order to become familiar with the position	

51st Company Machine Gun Corps

Army Form C. 2118.

WAR DIARY
or
INTELLIGENCE SUMMARY.
(Erase heading not required.)

Place	Date	Hour	Summary of Events and Information	Remarks and references to Appendices
In the field	9th Sep.		On the afternoon of the 9th we commenced the relief which was completed by	
		7.p.m.	Company Headquarters in York Street. Ref Map. PROUVAIN. Ref. Map. H.17.c.2.6. Position of Guns as follows:- Reference PROUVAIN MAP 1/10000	
			Gun No 1 at I.14.c.0540. No 2 at I.14.c.0559. No 3 at I.14.a.7555.	
			" 4 at I.14.a.0590. " 5 at I.7.D.9515 " 9 at I.13.B.5520.	
			" 10 at I.13.B.3580 " 11 at I.7.D.0545 " 20 at H.18.B.9515	
			" 21 at H.12.D.7530 " 22 at H.12.D.7545 " 31 at H.18.a.8545	
			" 32 at H.18.a.7575 " 17 at I.19.a.3595 " 18 at I.13.c.1535	
			" 19 at I.13.c.0570 " 20 at H.18.B.9515 " 12 at H.7.B.2515	
			" 13 at H.17.B.2040. " 17 at H.11.c.8575 " 16 at H.11.c.9560.	
9/10			Guns No 17, 18, 19, and 20 were mounted by teams of 236 M.G. Coy.	
			We carried out the following indirect fire. Gun No 17 Target I.8.b.8515 - Tracks	
			Gun No 18 Target I.8.b.6060 - Tracks Gun No 21 Target I.2.D.7050 - Ho. Dos	
			Gun No. 22 Target I.2.D.7050 - Ho. Dos Gun No 31 Target I.8.B. Central - Tracks	
			Gun No 32 Target I.8.b.Central - Tracks. Total number of rounds fired 6000.	

Army Form C. 2118.

51st Company Machine Gun Corps

WAR DIARY
or
INTELLIGENCE SUMMARY.
(Erase heading not required.)

Instructions regarding War Diaries and Intelligence Summaries are contained in F. S. Regs., Part II. and the Staff Manual respectively. Title pages will be prepared in manuscript.

Place	Date	Hour	Summary of Events and Information	Remarks and references to Appendices
In the field	10/11		In co-operation with Artillery indirect fire was carried out as follows.	
			Gun No 17 on I.8.a.6090.	
			" 18 " I.8.a.7510.	
			" 19 } New Trench running from WORM to WINDMILL COPSE.	
			" 20 }	
			" 21 " I.8.d.3535.	
			" 22 " — "	
			" 31 " I.8.d.5035.	
			" 32 " I.8.d.8035.	
			Rate and rate of fire one minute bursts of intense fire at 10.30 pm and 11.6 pm then intermittently throughout the night. Total number of rounds fired 13,750.	
	11/12		The same guns fired and the same targets were engaged as on night of 10/11. No of rounds fired 12,500. Firing was carried out intermittently throughout the night.	
	12/13		Indirect fire was carried out as follows.	
			Gun No 17. Target I.9.a.6090 to } New Trench	
			" 18 " I.8.a.7510 }	

Army Form C. 2118.

51st Company Machine Gun Corps

WAR DIARY
or
INTELLIGENCE SUMMARY.
(Erase heading not required.)

Instructions regarding War Diaries and Intelligence Summaries are contained in F. S. Regs., Part II. and the Staff Manual respectively. Title pages will be prepared in manuscript.

Place	Date	Hour	Summary of Events and Information	Remarks and references to Appendices
In the field	12th/13th		Gun No. 19 } Target I 9 c 2.7. New work on XVII Corps	
			" 20 } Intelligence Summary No. 239	
			" 21 } I 8. d 3555 New Trench leading to	
			" 22 } COST TRENCH	
			" 31 " I 8 D 5035 New Trench from	
			" 32 " I 8 D 8035 WORM to COST TRENCH	
			Total number of rounds fired 9,000	
	13/14th		Indirect fire was carried out during the night as under:-	
			Gun No. 17 Target I 2 D 7.5.	
			" 18 " - . -	
			" 19 " I 9 a 5095	
			" 20 " I 9 a 3.7	
			" 21 " I 8 b 4545	
			" 22 " I 8 b 8.5.	
			" 31 " I 8 b 1525	
			" 32 " I 8 b 0530	

Army Form C. 2118.

51st Company Machine Gun Corps

WAR DIARY
or
INTELLIGENCE SUMMARY.
(Erase heading not required.)

Instructions regarding War Diaries and Intelligence Summaries are contained in F. S. Regs., Part II. and the Staff Manual respectively. Title pages will be prepared in manuscript.

Place	Date	Hour	Summary of Events and Information	Remarks and references to Appendices
In the field	13/14		All the above targets are tracks which were searched throughout the night as from information received from prisoners the enemy was effecting a relief. Total number of rounds fired 15000	
	15/16		Indirect fire was carried out during the night by the same guns & on the same targets as on the night of 13/14th. Number of rounds fired 15000	
	16/17		At 9pm on the night of the 16th inst. the 10th Sherwood Foresters carried out a raid on CRUST TRENCH in I.14.c with the object of killing Germans destroying dug-outs & obtaining identifications. The four guns in Intermediate Line I.2. I.3. I.6. 9. I.7. were moved up to the following positions Gun No 1 I.2 at I.13.c.2305 called 17a " 2 I.3 " I.13.c.22 - 18a " 3 I.6 " I.13.c.0585 - 19a " 4 I.7 " I.13.a.0570 - 20a The following guns co-operated with the artillery Gun No 17 Target CLOD TRENCH	

Army Form C. 2118.

51st Company Machine Gun Corps

WAR DIARY
or
INTELLIGENCE SUMMARY.
(Erase heading not required.)

Place	Date	Hour	Summary of Events and Information	Remarks and references to Appendices
In the field	16/17		Gun No. 17a Target CLOD TRENCH	
			" 18 Tracks from Scarpe in I.21.b	
			" 18a	
			" 19 Target CLAY TRENCH	
			" 19a Road in I.15.c.1	
			" 20 Bank in I.15.c & d	
			" 20a Road in I.15.c	
			" 21 Road in I.14.b & I.15.a	
			" 22 "	
			" 31 Hausa Wood	
			" 32 "	
			Rate of fire – Bursts of intense fire from Zero to Zero +15. Zero hour 9 pm	
			After Zero +15 17a 18a 19a & 20a were withdrawn to their battle emplacements	
			in Intermediate Line. Number of rounds fired 28,000.	
			The raid was successful prisoners being taken. A considerable number of	
			Germans were killed dug-outs and T.M. emplacements blown up.	

WAR DIARY
or
INTELLIGENCE SUMMARY

Army Form C. 2118.

51st Company Machine Gun Corps

Place	Date	Hour	Summary of Events and Information	Remarks and references to Appendices
In the field	16/17		At 12 midnight the 12th Manchester Regt carried out a raid on WIT and WOOL TRENCHES on I.2 a 9 with the same object as the raid of the 10th Sherwood Foresters. The following guns co-operated.	
			Gun No. 17) Traversing from I.8 to 2053 to	
			" 18) I.8.b.80.15 Track along road	
			" 19 Wavy Trench I.9 a 40.75 I.2 d 6.3	
			" 20 Traversing WHY Trench	
			Gun No. 21 Traversing searching WEAK Trench New work I.2 b 50.55	
			" 22 New work at I.3 a 2.5	
			" 31 Traverse WEASEL Trench	
			" 32 New work I.8 b 52-75	
			Rate of fire Zero to Zero+5 3 belts per gun per 3 minutes Z.05 to Z+35	
			3 belts per gun per 5 minutes	
			Zero+12 midnight 16/17th. Number of rounds fired 25,000	
			Total number of rounds fired during the night – 45,000	
	17/18		Indirect fire was carried out during the night :–	
			Gun No. 17 Target T.21 b 80.40) Tracks leading	
			" 18 " T.21 b 80.45) to River Scarpe	
			" 20 " I.9 a 28 New Trench from WEED	
			" 22 " I.14 b 5.5. New work in CANDY Trench	

51st Company Machine Gun Corps

Army Form C. 2118.

WAR DIARY
or
INTELLIGENCE SUMMARY.
(Erase heading not required.)

Place	Date	Hour	Summary of Events and Information	Remarks and references to Appendices
In the field	17/18th		Gun No. 19 Target I.9.c.2.8 New Trench from WORM	
			" 21 " I 14.b 45.60 " work in CANDY Trench	
			" 31 " I 14.b 65.35 } work in " "	
			" 32 " I 14.b 6740	
			Total number of rounds fired - 9,500.	
			During the day of the 18th section relief were carried out as follows	
			2/Lt Wright No. 4 Section changed places with Lt Duncan No. 1 Section	
			Lt Noble No. 2 Section changed places with Lt Jnathon No. 3 Section	
			2/Lt Mann relieved Lt Noble who returned to Headquarters	
			In cooperation with artillery the following indirect fire was carried	
			out on the morning of the 19th inst.	
18/19th			Gun No. 17 Target I 8.a 75.10 Tape at WILLOW	
			" 18 " I 15.c 2.5 New work CANDY & CYRIL	
			" 19 " I 15.c 8.9 Where GRID CLIFF & Bank meet road	
			" 20 " I 15.a 30.65 Where CLIFF crosses road	
			" 21 " I 14.b 45.60 New work	

51st Company Machine Gun Corps

Army Form C. 2118

WAR DIARY
or
INTELLIGENCE SUMMARY
(Erase heading not required.)

Place	Date	Hour	Summary of Events and Information	Remarks and references to Appendices
In the field	18/19		Gun No. 22 Target I 14 b 5.5 New work.	
			" 31 " I 14 b 6525 New work on CANDY.	
			" 32 " I 14 d 5025 Track Junction :-	
			Time & rate of fire :- Intense bursts of fire for one minute at 2-30 a.m. 2-45 a.m. 3-10 a.m. Indirect fire was carried out as follows. From dark until 2-30 a.m.	
			Gun No. 17 Target I 15 b 6.4 ⎫	
			" 18 " I 15. b 40.65 ⎬ Main cross roads.	
			" 19 " " " ⎭	
			" 20 " I 15 b 6.4	
			" 21 " I 9 e 6535 ⎫ Railway Road &	
			" 22 " " " ⎬ Trench Junction.	
			" 31 " I 8 d 6520 Tracks.	
			" 32 " I 8 d 9010 Trench along Railway.	
			Total number of rounds fired 10,000.	
	19/20		The same targets were engaged during the night so were fired on during the morning of the 19th inst. Total number of rounds fired 10,550.	

Army Form C. 2118

51st Company Machine Gun Corps

WAR DIARY
or
INTELLIGENCE SUMMARY
(Erase heading not required.)

Instructions regarding War Diaries and Intelligence Summaries are contained in F. S. Regs., Part II. and the Staff Manual respectively. Title Pages will be prepared in manuscript.

Place	Date	Hour	Summary of Events and Information	Remarks and references to Appendices
In the field	19/20		For the last two or three days the Enemy has shown considerable aerial activity - As a rule whenever except in ones when E.A have flown out of range A.A & Machine Gun fire have kept the behind their own lines.	
	20/21		Indirect fire was carried out during the night as follows	
			Gun No 17 Target I 15 b 6 4 ⎫	
			" 18 " I 15 b 40 65 ⎬ Plouvain Cross roads
			" 19 " — " — ⎭
			" 20 " I 15 b 6. 4 Railway Road 9
			" 21 " I 9 c 6535 Trench Junction
			" 22 " I 8 d 6520 Tracks
			" 31 " I 8 d 90 10 Trench along Railway
			Total number of rounds fired 10,500	
	21/22nd		Indirect fire was carried out during the night as follows :-	
			Gun No 17 Target I 21 & 8040 Tracks from Plouvain Road to Scarpe
			" 18 " I 15 b 4085 Plouvain Cross roads.
			" 19 " I 9 c 31 6 lay Trench
			" 20 " I 15 a 30. 65 Where CLIFF crosses PLOUVAIN.

WAR DIARY or INTELLIGENCE SUMMARY

Army Form C. 2118

51st Company Machine Gun Corps

Place	Date	Hour	Summary of Events and Information	Remarks and references to Appendices
In the field	21/22		Gun No. 21 Target I 8 b 45.45 Where tracks cross road	
			" 22 " " I 9 c 6535 Railway & Road junction	
			" 31 " " I 8 d 6520 Tracks at Windmill Copse	
			" 32 " " I 8 d 9010 WURZEL TRENCH	
			Intense bursts of fire at 2.30 a.m and 2.45 & 3.10 a.m, one minute intermittently throughout the night, both before & after the above times. Number of rounds fired – 15,000.	
	22/23		Indirect fire during the night was as follows.	
			Gun No. 17 Target I 14 b 8045 CLOD Trench	
			" 18 " " I 15 c 2.5 CANDY -- " --	
			" 19 " " I 9 c 3.1 CLAY -- " --	
			" 20 " " I 8 d 8505 WURZEL -- " --	
			" 21 " " I 15 a 3065 CLOD -- " --	
			" 22 " " I 8 d 3555 New Trench from OOST	
			" 31 " " I 8 d 6520 WINDMILL COPSE	
			" 32 " " I 8 a 8035 WALNUT Trench	
			Total number of rounds fired 9,500.	

Army Form C. 2118.

WAR DIARY
or
INTELLIGENCE SUMMARY.
(Erase heading not required.)

51st Company Machine Gun Corps

Instructions regarding War Diaries and Intelligence Summaries are contained in F. S. Regs., Part II. and the Staff Manual respectively. Title pages will be prepared in manuscript.

Place	Date	Hour	Summary of Events and Information	Remarks and references to Appendices
In the field	22/23rd		During the day of the 22nd inst. 236 Machine Gun Company withdrew their guns from Nos 17, 18, 19→20 Positions their Positions were then occupied by the four guns from I 2, I 3, I 6, & I 7, Positions on Intermediate line. The Intermediate line Positions were rested.	
			Lieut A R Fraser returned from leave.	
	23/24		The following Indirect fire was carried out during the night.	
			Gun N° 17 Target I 44.b 8045 CLOD Trench	
			" 18 " I 15.e 2-5 CANDY - " -	
			" 19 " I 9.c 3.1 CLAY - " -	
			" 20 " I 8.d 8505 WURZEL - " -	
			" 21 " I 15.a 3065 CLOD - " -	
			" 22 " I 8.d 3555 WALNUT - " -	
			" 31 " I 8.d 6520 WINDMILL COPSE	
			" 32 " I 8.d 8035 WALNUT Trench	
			Fire was kept up intermittently from dusk until 4.30 a.m. when no response to S.O.S signal the alarm guns invariably fired on the Southern Barrage lines and opened fire until the situation quietened at 5.15 a.m.	
			In addition to the above gun fire was opened by Guns N° 3, 4 & 5 in	

A5834 Wt. W4973/M687 750,000 8/16 D. D. & L. Ltd. Forms/C.2118/13

WAR DIARY or INTELLIGENCE SUMMARY

Army Form C. 2118.

51st Company Machine Gun Corps

Place	Date	Hour	Summary of Events and Information	Remarks and references to Appendices
In the field	23/24		Oxford Trench, & Gun No. 11 in Calico Trench. Total rounds fired during the night 19,000. During the afternoon & evening the 57th Inf Bde less 51st Machine Gun Coy and T.M. Batty were relieved by the 182nd Brigade.	
	24th		The 182nd Machine Gun Coy sent up one man for each gun team in order to get familiar with the ground. During the afternoon the 182nd Machine Gun Company relieved the 57th Machine Gun Coy. Relief was completed by 9-0 pm. 51st Machine Gun Coy marched back to billets in Arras.	
	25th		At 7-30 am Company with transport marched to Berneville where they spent the night.	
	26th		At 9-30 am Company with Transport marched with rest of Brigade. Our billets were at Lieucourt. Brigade being at Izengny. We arrived at Lieucourt at 2-30 p.m. Some information received from a Prisoner captured on the morning of the 24th the raid was carried out by Divisional Storm Troops.	

Army Form C. 2118.

57th Company Machine Gun Corps

WAR DIARY
or
INTELLIGENCE SUMMARY.

(Erase heading not required.)

Instructions regarding War Diaries and Intelligence Summaries are contained in F. S. Regs., Part II. and the Staff Manual respectively. Title pages will be prepared in manuscript.

Place	Date	Hour	Summary of Events and Information	Remarks and references to Appendices
In the field	26.9		consisting of one officer and 60 men assisted by small detachment of Pioneers. The enemy failed to reach our lines. The Pioneers explored & belonged to the Pioneers. The infantry were armed with Carbines & bombs & the Pioneers with bombs only. Company at Achements.	
	27/30		Training carried on with a Company re-equipped.	

30-9-18.

P. Harvey Wargh
Capt.
Commdg. 57th M.G. Coy.

Army Form C. 2118.

WAR DIARY
or
INTELLIGENCE SUMMARY.
(Erase heading not required.)

51 M.G. Coy Vol 21

51st Company Machine Gun Corps.

Instructions regarding War Diaries and Intelligence Summaries are contained in F. S. Regs., Part II. and the Staff Manual respectively. Title pages will be prepared in manuscript.

Place	Date	Hour	Summary of Events and Information	Remarks and references to Appendices
In the field	2/10/1917 Oct 3rd		Company marched to OPPY and carried out exercises with rest of Brigade. Transport left LIENCOURT at 5 pm and marched to SAULTY. Company & Transport entrained at SAULTY at 10.42 pm and arrived at PESELHOER Station at 10.0 am on the 4th where they went into SASCATOON Camp.	
	Oct 5th		Company & Transport left SASCATOON Camp at 3.45 pm and marched to HERZEELE arriving at 9.30 pm. Company went into billets and carried on with training. Eight men from each Battalion were attached to Company to assist in the carrying of ammunition.	
	5/6/7th		Company stayed in Billets at HERZEELE.	
	9th		Left thus on the 8th and marched to SASCATOON ST SIXTE AREA arriving at 9.30 pm. Roads very heavy owing to rain. At 6.30 am Company left SASCATOON Camp and entrained at INTERNATIONAL CORNER STATION for ELVERDINGHE (Belgian Map 28 N.W.) B.W. d.8.5. and camp at WHITE MILL B.W. d.4.5. Transport was brigaded & proceeded from SASCATOON CAMP to ELVERDINGHE by road, their lines were also at WHITEMILL. Company arrived in Camp at 10.30 am	
	10th		During the afternoon of the 10th the Company started to relieve the Guns of the 86th and 88th Machine Gun Companies of the 29th Division.	

A 5834. Wt. W4973/M687 750,000 8/16 D. D. & L. Ltd. Forms/C.2118/13

Army Form C. 2118.

51st Company Machine Gun Corps

WAR DIARY
or
INTELLIGENCE SUMMARY.
(Erase heading not required.)

Instructions regarding War Diaries and Intelligence Summaries are contained in F. S. Regs., Part II. and the Staff Manual respectively. Title pages will be prepared in manuscript.

Place	Date	Hour	Summary of Events and Information	Remarks and references to Appendices
In the field	Oct 9th		The positions of the Guns were as follows:—	
			Reference BROEMBEEK map edition 3 10,000	
			4 Guns under Lieut G Wright & 2/Lt J.D Mann N°. 4 Section	
			U.12.d.7.9.	
			U.12.d.6.9.	
			U.12.b.6.1.	
			U.12.b.6.3.	
			2 Guns under 2/Lieut A.C Noble N°.1 Section	
			U.12.d.9.4.	
			U.12.D.8.6.	
			2 Guns under Lieut A Duncan N°.1 Section	
			U.7.0.5.5.	
			2 Guns under Sgt Fox N°.2 Section	
			U.13.a.4.8.	
			2 Guns under 2/Lieut H.H Arnold N°.2 Section	
			U.18.d.4.4.	
			2 Guns under Sgt Dye N°.3 Section	
			U.19.a.8.2.	

WAR DIARY or INTELLIGENCE SUMMARY

Army Form C. 2118.

57th Company Machine Gun Corps

Place	Date	Hour	Summary of Events and Information	Remarks and references to Appendices
In the field	Oct 10		2 Guns under Lieut O.A. Jonathon and two teams of No 3 Section were left behind at Transport Line. Two Sub Sections took their guns up to TRAFALGAR Square Transport. LANGEMARKE by limbers the remaining Sections by Pack to MARTIN MILL. From these two places the guns were man handled. Guns, Tripods, Spare Barrels, first aid and case of 6 belts ammunitions were taken up by each gun team. On the night of the 10th/11th were in a Pill box in Coy H.Q. TRAFALGAR SQUARE LANGEMARKE U23.C.10.15. It was moved on the morning of the 11th to MARTINS MILL U22.04.5. Roads & tracks Roads from ELVERDINGHE to LANGEMARKE were in good condition considering the weather. Forward of LANGEMARKE the road to front line was practically impassable owing to the shell holes & mud. The other track up to the front line was the Railway which was very badly broken up by shell fire. Dispositions of Guns for the attack which took place on the morning of the 12/10/17. Six Guns were withdrawn to Barrage Positions at V18.c.2.8. Emplacements	
12				

Army Form C. 2118.

57th Company Machine Gun Corps

WAR DIARY
or
INTELLIGENCE SUMMARY.

(Erase heading not required.)

Instructions regarding War Diaries and Intelligence Summaries are contained in F. S. Regs., Part II. and the Staff Manual respectively. Title pages will be prepared in manuscript.

Place	Date	Hour	Summary of Events and Information	Remarks and references to Appendices
In the field	8/10/17		were made as well as it was possible in shell holes. This six guns were laid on S.O.S. lines 500 yds in front of the front line by 8.0 p.m. on the night of the 11/12th. About one hour before ZERO hour the front line guns were withdrawn to the forming up position in front of the road running from U.12.b.3.6. through TRANQUILLE HOUSE, CONDIE HOUSE, to U.13.a.30.35. Guns were allotted to Battalions as follows:- 2 Guns under 2/Lieut J.D. Mann to 8th South Staffs " " 2 " " Lieut G. Wright to 4th Lincolnshire Regt " " 2 " " 2/Lieut A.C. Noble to 10th Sherwood Foresters " " 2 " " Lieut A. Duncan " 12th Oct. Zero was 5.25 a.m. morning of the 12th October. The machine guns kept close up to the leading infantry and which pushed to to the right place. The enemy offered little or no resistance except on the front of the 8th South Staffs Regt at ADEN HOUSE which offered a stubborn resistance the advance of this flank was	

"57th Company Machine Gun Corps"

Army Form C. 2118.

WAR DIARY
or
INTELLIGENCE SUMMARY.
(Erase heading not required.)

Instructions regarding War Diaries and Intelligence Summaries are contained in F.S. Regs., Part II. and the Staff Manual respectively. Title pages will be prepared in manuscript.

Place	Date	Hour	Summary of Events and Information	Remarks and references to Appendices
In the field	Oct 12/1917.		On the right of ADEN HOUSE the two guns with the 8th South Staffs eventually got into position near TURENNE CROSSING at vic 9025 & vic 95.25 both with excellent fields of fire the latter in position to command ADEN HOUSE in case of necessity. One of the guns going forward with the 8th South Staffs eventually got into position with one man Pte Fleming carrying Gun & 2 boxes of ammunition. Of the two guns went forward on the left flank of the 4th Lincs under Lieut. to Wright. One of these teams met with casualties at the start of the attack only two of the team being left. The man carrying the Tripod & the N.C.O. in charge of the team these two pushed on to the final objective where they found the one gun under 2/Lieut G.B. Mann with only one gunner left. The other gun under Lieut. to Wright reached TURENNE CROSSING & took up a position thus commanding the Railway & the VISFWEBEN ROAD. The two guns allotted to the right flank of the 4th Lincolns	

Army Form C. 2118.

51st Company Machine Gun Corps

WAR DIARY
or
INTELLIGENCE SUMMARY.
(Erase heading not required.)

Place	Date	Hour	Summary of Events and Information	Remarks and references to Appendices
In the field	12/10/17		went under the command of 2/Lieut A.O. Botte who unfortunately became a casualty before the attack. The N.C.O. in charge pushed forward on to TAUBE FARM according to instructions. Resistance was offered at this farm so he mounted two guns in rear of it. The two guns with the 10th Sherwood Forester pushed right on until the first wave of the infantry to GRAVEL FARM where they took up positions as followed. V4 b 8.1.9 V8.a.1.9. One gun enfilading the front & TURENNE CROSSING the other gun enfilading the MEMLING FARM. Ammunition 6 Belt boxes were taken up by each gun team this was made up to an average of 16 belt boxes per gun repeatedly. Before the attack took place, the guns that reached the final objective carried with an average of 1 6 Belt boxes per gun. Dumps of S.A.A. there were established at "jumping off places" but owing to the open nature of the country it was a matter of extreme difficulty to git back to these dumps on account of enemies machine gun fire also owing to casualties, few men could be spared from the gun teams	

WAR DIARY or INTELLIGENCE SUMMARY

Army Form C. 2118.

57th Company Machine Gun Corps

Place	Date	Hour	Summary of Events and Information	Remarks and references to Appendices
In the field	2/10/17		consequently ammunition had to be resent for any counter attacks that might take place. It was arranged that ration parties & runners carry up battalions, as the carrying up of S.A.A in bow was out of the question owing to the depletion of the personnel. The Company was relieved on the night of the 13th & it was arranged that each time of the incoming Company should carry up an extra 1000 S.A.A per gun. Barrage Guns Machine guns of the 19 Machine Gun Corps of the Division were employed on barrage as follows: 51st M.G Coy 6 guns forming "A" Battery, 60th M.G Coy 6 guns forming "B" Battery, 52nd M.G Coy 6 guns forming "C" Battery, 236 M.G Coy 12 guns forming "D" & "E" Batteries. These guns were formed into two groups, right & left groups each under a group commander, both under the Six Machine Gun Officer, each group was sub divided into Batteries of 6 guns each. Each Battery was under the command of an officer appointed as Battery commander by his Brigade Machine Gun Coy commander. The barrage of	

57th Company Machine Gun Corps

Army Form C. 2118.

WAR DIARY
or
INTELLIGENCE SUMMARY

(Erase heading not required.)

Place	Date	Hour	Summary of Events and Information	Remarks and references to Appendices
In the field	12/10/17		"B" Battery was carried out according to D.M.G.O. instructions as under:-	

Target	Range	Q E	Elevation on own troops	Zero Time Zero 0+8+	Clock Time	Rate of fire
No 1	1600	2° 35'	26*	0 to 8	5.25 to 5.33	1 Belt per four minutes
" 2	1700	3°	31.7	8 to 16	5.33 to 5.41	
" 3	1800	3° 21'	39.4	16 to 24	5.41 to 5.49	
" 4	1900	3° 47'	45	24 to 40	5.49 to 6.5	
" 5	2000	4° 16'	53	40 to 48	6.5 to 6.13	
" 6	2100	4° 48'	63	48 to 56	6.13 to 6.21	
" 7	2200	5° 22'	71.7	56 to 64	6.21 to 6.29	
" 8	2300	6°	83.3	64 to 72	6.29 to 6.57	
" 9	2400	6° 41'	96	92 to 100	6.57 to 7.51	
" 10	2500	7° 24'	111	100 to 108	7.5 to 7.13	

Fire was carried on from 5.25 a.m to 7.13 at the rate of one belt per gun per four minutes.

Rate of fire for SOS Barrage 1 belt per gun per minute till our artillery Barrage well on, then slacken to 1 belt per four minutes. The SOS went up about 5.0 p.m on the Evening of the 12th & all the Guns

WAR DIARY
or
INTELLIGENCE SUMMARY.

Army Form C. 2118.

51st Company Machine Gun Corps

(Erase heading not required.)

Instructions regarding War Diaries and Intelligence Summaries are contained in F.S. Regs., Part II and the Staff Manual respectively. Title pages will be prepared in manuscript.

Place	Date	Hour	Summary of Events and Information	Remarks and references to Appendices
In the field	12/10/17		The Barrage Group opened fire within 60 seconds putting down a curtain of fire 500ˣ from the front line. Ammunition. On night of the 11/12th an S.A.A. dump of 50000 rounds was established at U.17.c Y.9. beside the junction of railway & the BROEMBEEK for the Barrage guns. On the night of the 12/13th Mules were got up again with 48 Belt Boxes and 30 more boxes of S.A.A. Returns Each team took into the line two days rations & water, and out down to Coy H.Q. for further supplies which were brought up from Transport line by Pack Mules. The attack was a great success & all objectives were reached. The conditions could hardly have been worse the whole of the ground was torn up by shell fire & there was no cover with the exception of isolated pill boxes. Owing to the recent heavy rain the ground was quagmire.	
	13/14th		On the night of the 13th & 14th this Company was relieved by 50th M.G. Coy with the exception of the 6 barrage guns which were withdrawn.	

WAR DIARY
INTELLIGENCE SUMMARY

Army Form C. 2118.

71st Company Machine Gun Corps

Place	Date	Hour	Summary of Events and Information	Remarks and references to Appendices
In the field	13th & 14th		Relief was completed by 6.30 am 14th. Company returned to WHITETHORN CAMP. In the afternoon of the 14th the Company moved to CARIBOU CAMP (BERGUM) (28 NW) a.n.a. 9.3.	
	16th		On the 16th the Company left camp and entrained at ELVERDINGHE, detraining at PROVEN. Marched to PERTH CAMP near PROVEN. Transport moved by road. Arrived in camp at 2.0 pm. 2/Lt J.D. Mann proceeded on leave to U.K. on this date. 2/Lt T.M. Griff returned from leave. The following casualties occurred during this tour in the Trenches 10/10/14 to 16th October.	
	18th		No. 103045 Pte Grant H. Killed in action 12/10/17 No. 6209 L/Cpl Rabin J. Killed in action 12/10/17 Pte Hurst S. Killed in action 12/10/17 89289. L/Cpl Dakin J. Killed in action 12/10/17 13626 Sgt. Northington. Killed in action 12/10/17. 2/Lt A. O'Neill Wounded in action 13/10/17 No.84736. Pte McKenzie A. Wounded in action 12/10/17 No. 36643 Pte Foster E. Wounded in action 12/10/17 No. 70831. Pte Charles D. Wounded in action 11/10/17 No. 6949. L/Cpl Lee B.T. 11049. Pte Rushton C. R10311. Pte Green K No. 3619. Pte Hadley F. No. 36335 Pte Duncan A.B. No. 30702 Sgt Neeler B. No. 53969. Pte Pattinson W. No. 61163 Pte Johnson G. (Wounded in action) 12/10/19. No. 95145. Pte Alloway G. No. 67951 Pte Kirk H. Wounded in action 13/10/17 36974 Sgt Fox A.E. Wounded and remained at duty 12/10/17. No.101794. No.35179 Lt Finnigan M. Mann J.T. Wounded and remained at duty 12/10/17. No.35179 Lt Finnigan M. Wounded and remained at duty 13/10/17	

Army Form C. 2118.

51st Company Machine Gun Corps.

WAR DIARY
INTELLIGENCE SUMMARY
(Erase heading not required.)

Instructions regarding War Diaries and Intelligence Summaries are contained in F.S. Regs., Part II. and the Staff Manual respectively. Title pages will be prepared in manuscript.

Place	Date	Hour	Summary of Events and Information	Remarks and references to Appendices
In the Field			The following casualties occurred to attached men from Battalions as shewn below No 71218 Pte Blisdale T wounded in action 12/10/17. No 80072 Pte Mitchen D wounded in action 12/10/17. No 473 m Pte Jenkins A.E. Wounded in action 12/10/17. No 367915 Pte Chambers W. Wounded in action 10/10/17. These men all belong to the 10th Batt Notts & Derby Regiment. No 41494 Pte Candler W.H. Wounded in action No 41524 Pte Hill A wounded in action. No 23096 Pte Buckley L Wounded in action 43/25 Pte Turner F.W. No 32333 Pte Hollouts E. Missing 12/10/1917. Attached from the 8th Batt South Staffordshire Regiment. No 23100 Pte Parfitt E. Wounded in action 14/10/17 No 27615 Pte Prentice W. Wounded in action 13/10/17 (1st Batt (11.G.Y) Border Regiment.	
	16th/20th		Company carried out training Commenced re-equipping at Pilch Camp near PROVEN.	
	21st		Company with rest of Brigade embussed at PROVEN at 6 a.m for LICQUES. and marched to CLERQUES. and LE HANEL where company was billetted. Transport left Pilch Camp on the 20th and proceeded to CLERQUES by road.	
	22nd/23rd 24th		Company at CLERQUES carried on with training Six guns and teams under 2/Lt Arnold & 2/Lt J.W. Higgins left for GROSSE PANELLE to train for barrage work under D.M.G.O.	
	25th		Company left CLERQUES Entrained at AUDRICQ arriving PROVEN PARANA CAMP at 11.0 p.m Transport travelled by light train and arrived about 6.0am on 26th inst	

Army Form C. 2118.

7th Company, Machine Gun Corps

WAR DIARY
INTELLIGENCE SUMMARY
(Erase heading not required.)

Place	Date	Hour	Summary of Events and Information	Remarks and references to Appendices
In the Field	25th		Capt. P.F. Haugh proceeded on leave to England on this date. Lieut. J.M. Richardson assumed command of the Company.	
	26th		Company entrained at PROVEN 10-30 a.m., detrained at BOESINGHE and marched to BOESINGHE Camp. Transport proceeded by road to Box Camp near ELVERDINGHE.	
	27th		During the afternoon the Company relieved 10 guns in the line of the 35th Division. Four guns in forward positions Map Ref. BIXSCHOOTE 1/10,000 U.5.B.1.5. U.5.d.2.4. U.5.d.7.4. U.6.c.3.6. Two guns at U.11.c.55-05. U.11.c.4.3.10 forming E group with S.O.S. barrage line road running from our left flank starting at 0.35.c.9.3. Four guns at PASCAL FARM U.12.a.55-30. U.12.d.60.30. U.12.d.00.30. U.12.d.80.40. forming D group with S.O.S. barrage line, 0.36.d.30.25. to 0.36.c.7.3. Relief started at 5-30 p.m. and was completed by 10-30 p.m. Two half boxes only per gun were taken up to Signal Farm U.21.d.20.05. into the line, there being a plentiful supply in the position. Rations and water were also taken up. During the night of the 28th/29th indirect fire was carried out as follows. Two guns of E group fired on road on the right of E group fired 1500. Two guns of D group fired on 0.35.c.9.3. number of rounds fired 1500. to 0.36.D.30.25. to 0.36.D.7.3. Number of rounds fired 4,000. Three targets were the S.O.S. lines for the two groups. During our tour	

Army Form C. 2118.

51st Company Machine Gun Corps

WAR DIARY
or
INTELLIGENCE SUMMARY.
(Erase heading not required.)

Instructions regarding War Diaries and Intelligence Summaries are contained in F.S. Regs., Part II. and the Staff Manual respectively. Title pages will be prepared in manuscript.

Place	Date	Hour	Summary of Events and Information	Remarks and references to Appendices
In the field	29.		On the line there was no infantry action, but considerable Artillery action on both sides including a large number of gas shells. During the afternoon the four forward guns and the two gun forming E group were relieved by 6 guns of the 104 Machine Gun Company. The remaining four guns of D group being relieved by four guns of B 24th Machine Gun Company. Relief completed by 10 p.m. Company marched to BOESINGHE Camp and stayed the night there.	
	30.		Company entrained at BOESINGHE at 9.0 a.m. for PROVEN. Daranh Camp P.S. Area. Transport left Bov Camp 10.30 a.m. and arrived at PROVEN. 2.30 p.m. Owing to number of casualties sustained by other Machine Gun Companies in this transport on the roads up to the line, it was decided to man-handle the guns etc. Carrying parties were available for this purpose, as we only took four men per gun into the line there being no intention of an attack by our troops during this period. Aerial activity. Enemy air craft were very active considerable numbers of aeroplanes flying low and firing on troops in the front line. During the night the enemy persistently bombed the back areas. We had no casualties during the day.	
	31.		There was very little doing and nothing of	

Peter Nelson Capt.
Commanding
51 Machine Gun Company.

Army Form C. 2118.

51st Company Machine Gun Corps

WAR DIARY
INTELLIGENCE SUMMARY

51 M G Coy

Place	Date	Hour	Summary of Events and Information	Remarks and references to Appendices
In the field	Nov 1st 1917		Company and Transport left PARANA Camp P.S. and PROVEN and marched to HARDIFORT, near CASSEL. Map Reference Sheet 24 Belgium & Part of France I.23.D.5.4.	
	1/7th	8 a.m.	Company re-equipped and carried on with training at HARDIFORT.	
			Company and Transport marched to PROVEN and went into PILEH Camp Map Reference Sheet 24 Belgium and Part of France F15.B.8.8.	
	9/13th		Training carried on. Capt. D.H. Haugh rejoined Company from leave to U.K. on the 10th and again took over command of Company.	
	13th		Company entrained at PROVEN for ELVERDINGHE, MORTAR Camp B15 & 2.8 (Sheet 28 N.W.) LANGEMARCK II AREA. Lieut A. M. Richardson proceeded on leave to U.K. on this date.	
	14th		Training carried on as far as possible. Two Anti Aircraft positions prepared and Guns mounted.	
	14/18th		Training carried on. Lieut O.A. Jonathon admitted to Hospital on the 16th. Capt D H Haugh appointed D. M. G. O. during the absence of Major Calder on leave to U.K. Lieut A.R. Troar assumes command Lieut A Duncan and 2/Lieut J. D. Mann took admitted to Hospital sick.	
	18th			

Army Form C. 2118.

51st Company Machine Gun Corps

WAR DIARY
or
INTELLIGENCE SUMMARY.
(Erase heading not required.)

Instructions regarding War Diaries and Intelligence Summaries are contained in F.S. Regs., Part II. and the Staff Manual respectively. Title pages will be prepared in manuscript.

Place	Date	Hour	Summary of Events and Information	Remarks and references to Appendices
In the field	Nov 19/1917		Company relieved 50th Machine Gun Company on the line. Headquarters were at DROP HOUSES, LANGEMARCK, U.23.B.4.0 (BIXSCHOOTE). There were seven Guns in the line altogether, Support line positions numbered 1 to 7 from the left. N° 1 Gun Position V.Y.a.5.6. " 2 " " TAUBE FARM. V.Y.a.Y.0 " 3 " " V.Y.6.2.3 " 4) " " { SENEGAL FARM " 5) " " { V.Y.C.9.2 " 6 " " V.13.6.44 " 7 " " STRING HOUSES V.13.d.4.7 Map Reference (SCHAAP BALIE) Two Guns were kept back at Headquarters to replace any casualty in Guns that might arise, also a reserve of 20 Belt boxes, but none of these were needed. The Company suffered two casualties during relief on Nov 19th as follows:-	

WAR DIARY
INTELLIGENCE SUMMARY
Army Form C. 2118.

51st Company Machine Gun Corps

Place	Date	Hour	Summary of Events and Information	Remarks and references to Appendices
In the field	Nov 19/11/17		41502 Pte Annis E. Killed in Action. 10482 Pte Jones A.H. Wounded in Action. Both the above were attached for duty with this Company from the 8th Batt South Staffordshire Regt. No operations were carried out except the usual Patrolling by our own troops during the six days the Company were in the line. Enemy artillery fairly active on tracks and roads. The low number of casualties sustained is probably due to the fact that there being no trenches men were scattered in shell holes, thus affording no continuous mark for Enemy's artillery. Enemy Aeroplanes showed a good deal of activity dropping bombs on P.Ll troops, also flying very low and firing M.G. Guns. Hot food was sent up to the men in the line daily in special air jacket food containers, with fair success. The teams were relieved in the line (Inter Section Relief) on the 22nd each gun team mounting of 4 O.Rs.	

Army Form C. 2118.

57th Company Machine Gun Corps

WAR DIARY
or
INTELLIGENCE SUMMARY
(Erase heading not required.)

Place	Date	Hour	Summary of Events and Information	Remarks and references to Appendices
In the field	19/11/1917		First relief 2/Lt. T.M. Tripp in charge of numbers 1, 2, and 3 Gun Positions and Sgt Young in charge of 4, 5, 6, and 7 Gun Positions. Both Lieut O.A. Jmather and Lieut A. Duncan were evacuated sick to CCS on this date and struck off the strength of the Company.	
	20th		Second Relief (Inter Section Relief) Sgt Clarke in charge of numbers 1, 2, & 3 Gun Positions and 2/Lieut H. Arnold in charge of 4, 5, 6, & 7 Gun Positions	
	22nd		The Company was relieved on the line by 52nd Machine Gun Coy. Relief complete by 6.30 p.m. Relief was carried out at dusk. Teams Proceeded to Transport lines where a hot meal awaited them and then marched to CARDOEN Camp. Map Reference	
	23rd		A.18.B.0.4. (Sheet 28 NW) and joined remainder of Company. Three Officers reinforcements arrived from Base Depot. 2/Lieut H.G. Rowles, 2/Lt R.B. Robertson and 1/2 Lt R.H. Yingham.	

Army Form C. 2118.

WAR DIARY
INTELLIGENCE SUMMARY.

51st Company Machine Gun Corps

Instructions regarding War Diaries and Intelligence Summaries are contained in F. S. Regs., Part II. and the Staff Manual respectively. Title pages will be prepared in manuscript.

(Erase heading not required.)

Place	Date	Hour	Summary of Events and Information	Remarks and references to Appendices
In the field	26/30 Apr 1917		Training carried on at CARDOEN CAMP.	
	29th		Lieut F. M. Richardson rejoined Company from leave to U.K.	

A. Crown Lt. ?
Commanding
51 Machine Gun Company.

51st Company Machine Gun Corps

WAR DIARY
INTELLIGENCE SUMMARY
Army Form C. 2118.

Place	Date	Hour	Summary of Events and Information	Remarks and references to Appendices
Lechilel	Dec 20th		At O16 c 1.3. R/Co. Hqrs 57 C. Relief complete by 3.30 p.m. N/Lt F.N. Arnold proceeded on leave to England.	
	21.		The Company relieved 10 guns of the no 8 M.G. Coy. + 6 guns of the 191st Coy. in the line positions as follows :— R/Co Hqrs MARCOING Secteur. Coy H.Q. K15.a.2.1. 2 guns K17.b.5.6. 2guns K16.b.5.9. 2guns K10.c.7.1. 2 – K22.b.5.7. 2guns K18.c.1.9. 2guns K10.c.7.b 2guns K10.d.5.2.	
			Relief complete by 10 midn— transport remained at O16 c 1.3 until 23rd Dec. Lt Haggie returned from leave.	
	23/24		Two guns at K10 c 7.1 fired during the night at apparent to GILAIN COURT Number of rounds = 3000. Transport moved from O16 c 1.3. to BERTINCOURT.	
	24/25		Shurst fire during the night as follows :—	
			2 Guns @ K10 c 7.1. on E 29 d 3.2. + E30 c 8.2. Number of rounds fired = 8000	
			2 — @ K22.b.5.7. on K5.d.4.3. + K5.d.7.6.	
			2 — @ K10 c 7.1. on E 29.d.3.2. + E32.c.3.2. 2 Guns at K22.b.5.7. on K5.d.4.3. + K5.d.7.5. Number of rounds fired = 10000.	
	25/26		2 — @ K16.b.1.9 on K6.a.5.4. + K6.b.7.7.	
			2 — @ K10 c 7.1. on E29.d.3.2. + E30.C.3.2. 2 guns at K18.c.1.9. on K6.a.6.4.+ K6.a.7.7.	
	26/27		During the day of 26th night 26/27 & the morning of the 27 the enemy shelled the MARCOING Secteur heavily. We had the following casualties :—	
			KILLED Sgt RILEY E. No 3730	
			WOUNDED Pte CHAMBERS A. 60012. Cpl DEMPSEY P. 10768.	
	27/28		Shurst fire was carried out during the night as follows :— 2 Guns at K10 c 7.1. on E.29.d.3.1. + E30.c.3.1. 2 Guns at K22.b.5.7. + K5.d.4.3. 2 Guns at K16.d.4.7. on K6.a.5.4. + K6.a.8.5. Number of rounds fired = 6000. K6.c.7.6.	

Coy No. K15.d.2.1. N/a MARCOING

WAR DIARY or INTELLIGENCE SUMMARY

Army Form C. 2118.

Place	Date	Hour	Summary of Events and Information	Remarks and references to Appendices
	Nov 28		In the evening the Officers of the Company were relieved by the 236th M.G.Coy. Relief commenced at 6pm & was completed by 10pm. Company marched to TRESCAULT & TRESCAULT occupied. Dug out positions at Q.4.c.5.6. Kyde House H.Q. Transport remained at BEAUMETZ.	
	29/31		Company carried on with Forward Reconnaissance & on the evening of the 30th the Coy the Enemy on the right of the 36th Division was retiring & as retiring was very active especially on the support position. Coy the Hindenburg Support line was heavily shelled. Coy Co. relieved Capt. Kerr & Coy de H of the Tanks & Lieut. Cox also Came down. Coy was a Rein-fest during the bombardment. Lad rations were brought up to the Trenches in Lorries. In excellent condition. During the day night TRESCAULT was shelled intermittently.	

D.K. Kerr Capt.
Commanding
91 Machine Gun Company

1-1-18

SECRET.

7TH (WESTMORLAND AND CUMBERLAND YEOMANRY) BN. BORDER REGT.,

WAR DIARY

FOR

JANUARY

1918.

51st Company Machine Gun Corps

WAR DIARY
or
INTELLIGENCE SUMMARY

Army Form C. 2118.

51 M G Coy
Vol 24

Place	Date	Hour	Summary of Events and Information	Remarks and references to Appendices
In the field	Jan 1st 1918		Company trained and re-equipped at TRESCAULT (See 3"'e)	
	2nd/4th		On the night of the 4th/5th Company relieved A & B Grayhoof Machine Guns of the 2nd Division in the line H.Q. at K.14 b.13. Transport moved to SMALL WOOD in I 36.d.9.0 refrence map 57c The Gun positions taken over were Refrence map 57c HERMIES 1/10,000	
			Company Headquarters K.14 b.1.3.	
			2 Guns K. 8. b. 2.3	
			2 " K 9 a. 9.5	
			4 " K 9 c. 5.8.	
			4 " K 15 d. 2.8	
			2 " K 14 d 2.6	
			2 " K 13 b. 60.95	
			Relief was completed by 10 pm 4-1-18. During the night indirect fire was carried out on the approaches from GRAINCOURT & on CANAL.	
			Four Guns fired 3000 rounds as follows:—	
			1 Gun on trench K 4 b 4.9 to K.4 b 5.5	
			1 " " K 4 a 2.0 to K 4 a 15.45	
			1 " " CANAL from K 3 d 2.5	

WAR DIARY or INTELLIGENCE SUMMARY

Army Form C. 2118.

71st Company Machine Gun Corps

Place	Date	Hour	Summary of Events and Information	Remarks and references to Appendices
In the field	Jan 6/17		Indirect fire was carried out during the night as follows:-	
			4 Guns at K.15.d.2.8.	
			1 " in trench K.11.b.0.0. to K.4.b.5.5.	
			1 " — K.4.a.2.0 to K.10.c.6.45	
			1 " on CANAL from K.3.d.2.5 to K.3 Central.	
			1 " — E.29.c.2.1 to E.29.c.0.5.	
			2 " at K.14.d.6.6. searching K.2.a & K.2.c.	
			Rounds fired 4,500.	
	7/8/		Indirect fire was carried out during the night as follows:-	
			4 Guns at K.15.d.2.8.	
			1 " in trench K.4.b.4.0. to K.4.b.5.5.	
			1 " — K.4.a.2.0 to K.4.a.15-95	
			1 " on CANAL K.3.d.2.5 to K.3 Central.	
			1 " — E.29.c.2.1 to E.29.c.0.5	
			2 " at K.14.d.6.6. searching K.2.a & K.2.c.	
			Number of rounds fired 4,600.	
			The following alterations to Gun positions have been made to date.	
			2 Guns K.9.a.9.5. to 1 Gun K.9.b.1.5. 1 Gun K.9.a.Y.5.50	
			2 Guns at K.8.b.2.3. to 1 Gun K.8.d.6095 + 1 Gun K.8.b.6.4500.	
			2 Guns at K.9.c.5.8. to 1 Gun 1 Gun at K.9.a.1.5. + 1 Gun to K.8.d.80.95	

51st Company Machine Gun Corps

Army Form C. 2118.

WAR DIARY
or
INTELLIGENCE SUMMARY.
(Erase heading not required.)

Place	Date	Hour	Summary of Events and Information	Remarks and references to Appendices
In the field	2/9/18		The following intrusts fire was carried out during the night.	
			2 Guns at K.15.d.2.8 on tank K.4.b.2.0 to K.4.b.5.5	
			1 " " " K.4a.2.0. to K.4a.15.45.	
			2 Guns at K.14.d.6.6 searching K.2.a. and K.2.c.	
			Number of rounds fired 3000.	
			2 Guns at K.15.d.2.8 were moved to K.10.c.40.85 and K.10.c.10.95.	
			The disposition of Guns is now as follows:-	
			S1 at K.10.c.40.85	
			S2 " K.10.c.10.85	
			S3 " K.9.b.1.5	
			S4 " K.9.a.45.60	
			S5 " K.9.a.1.44	
			S6 " K.9.d.80.95	
			S7 " K.8.d.60.95.	
			S8 " K.8.c.45.00.	
			R1 " K.15.b.6.6.	
			R2 " K.15.b.0.4	
			R3 " K.9.c.40.95	
			R4 " K.15.a.20.65	
			R5 " K.14.d.30.85	
			R6 " K.14.b.13.28.	
			R7 " K.14.a.83.60	
			R8 " K.8.c.32.01	

Army Form C. 2118.

51st Company Machine Gun Corps

WAR DIARY
or
INTELLIGENCE SUMMARY.
(Erase heading not required.)

Instructions regarding War Diaries and Intelligence Summaries are contained in F.S. Regs., Part II and the Staff Manual respectively. Title pages will be prepared in manuscript.

Place	Date	Hour	Summary of Events and Information	Remarks and references to Appendices
In the field	9/10		The following indirect fire was carried out during the night as follows.	
	10/11		R.1. Gun on road K3 L64 to E27 L49. Number of rounds fired 2370. Indirect fire was carried out during the night as under— R1 ⎫ Searching and enfilade by R2 ⎬ K4 d 8.6 R4 ⎭ K5 c 20.55 K6 d 25.20 K11 c 6.5 Number of rounds fired 2070.	
	10/11		Under Section rifles was carried out during the afternoon. 2/Lt Routes & No 3 Section relieved N.M. Section (Lt Wright proceeded on leave) 1/Lt Higgins went to Transport Lines his place being taken by Lieut. Ralph.	
	11/12		No indirect fire was carried out during the night. The teams being employed in the laying out of new S.O.S. Barrage lines.	
	12/13		5700 Rounds were fired during the night on CANAL Tracks & roads by Guns number R2. R4. 6.	
	13/14		4100 rounds were fired during the night by Guns R2. R4 6. upon enemy approaches.	
	14/15		6500 rounds were fired during the night by Guns R2. R4 516. upon enemy approaches. 2/Lt Beamy took over command of 51+52 guns in WATSON TRENCH.	
	15/16		7000 rounds were fired during the night by Guns R2. R4. R5. & R6. upon enemy approaches.	

WAR DIARY
INTELLIGENCE SUMMARY

Army Form C. 2118.

51st Company Machine Gun Corps

Instructions regarding War Diaries and Intelligence Summaries are contained in F.S. Regs., Part II. and the Staff Manual respectively. Title pages will be prepared in manuscript.

Place	Date	Hour	Summary of Events and Information	Remarks and references to Appendices
In the field	16/1/17		In cooperation with the Artillery we fired during the night as follows:— Guns R1, R2 on trenches in K.4.b. Guns R4, R5 on trenches in K.4.d.	
			Times & Rate of Fire	
			R1 & R2 Guns 6.15pm, 7.40pm, 9 & 10.40pm. R4 & R5 6.45pm & 8.45pm. Intense bursts of fire for one minute afterwards intermittently throughout the night. Total number of rounds fired 10,000.	
	17/1/17		4000 rounds were fired during the night by Guns R2, R4, R5 & R6 on enemy approaches.	
	18/1/17		5000 rounds were fired during the night by Guns R2, R4, R5, & R6, on enemy approaches.	
	19/20th		During the relief of Infantry Battalions only 2000 rounds were fired during the night. The Guns that fired were R2 & R4.	
	20/1/17		On the 21st the Company was relieved by 58th M.G. Coy. Relief complete by 6.30 pm. The Company marched to HERMIES & entrained for HAPLINCOURT and went into camp at O.4.b.2.d. (one of Camp SANDERS). RATIONS were taken up the line by limber, by road as K.31.b.7.5. thence into CANAL, by ramp along CANAL to K.14.d.90.65. Roads & CANAL were in good condition.	

Defence W.D.
2/1/1.

51st Company Machine Gun Corps.

Army Form C. 2118.

WAR DIARY
or
INTELLIGENCE SUMMARY.
(Erase heading not required.)

Instructions regarding War Diaries and Intelligence Summaries are contained in F.S. Regs., Part II. and the Staff Manual respectively. Title pages will be prepared in manuscript.

Place	Date	Hour	Summary of Events and Information	Remarks and references to Appendices
In the field	21st		WEATHER. For the first 8 days the ground was hard & conditions on the line good, the first shown changed to a thaw for the remainder of the tour which, accompanied by rain made the trenches practically impassable in places. On account of the quick change of temperature & the consequent mud & water in the trenches there were a considerable number of cases of trench feet in the Brigade. Every precaution was taken. A sock drying room was opened at HERNIES where wet socks could be exchanged for dry ones. Gum boots which were worn could also the sent there for drying.	
	22/23 26th		From the 23rd to the 26th Company was at SANDERS CAMP Ry Sye Map D.14.d.5d. The Company relieved the 50th M.G. Coy in the right divisional sector of the line during the afternoon & evening. The Transport with Guns & Rations went by road. The Company entrained on light railway detraining at Q.2.a.5.5. and marched to Company Headquarters. Relief was completed by 8.55 p.m. Transport remained at VELU WOOD J.31.c.5.3. Ry Map 57c. The following are the positions taken up in the line. Reference BENICOURT 1/10,000 Coy H.Q. K.15.d.9.1.	

Army Form C. 2118.

51st Company Machine Gun Corps

WAR DIARY
INTELLIGENCE SUMMARY.
(Erase heading not required.)

Place	Date	Hour	Summary of Events and Information	Remarks and references to Appendices
In the field.	26/9		Nº 4 Position at K 10 d 98.60	
			" 7 " " K 10 d 25.45	
			" 8 " " K 10 d 17.55	
			" 5 " " K 16 b 35.65	
			" 6 " " K 16 b 35.75	
			" 12 " " K 16 b 4.9	
			" 15 " " K 10 c 4.1	
			" 16 " " K 10 c 40.15	
			" 9 " " K 16 d 45.50	
			" 10 " " K 16 d 6.6	
			" 13 " " K 22 b 45.85	
			" 14 " " K 22 b 5.8	
			" 1 " " K 17 b 5.6	
			" 2 " " K 17 b 4.6	
			" 3 " " K 16 c 55.65	
			" 11 " " K 16 c 60.65	
	27/9		These were eight Guns with Barrage lines and eight Guns with direct fire. During the night we carried out indirect fire on approaches to GRAINCOURT with 13. 14. 15 and 16 Guns. Number of rounds fired 4,000.	

Coy Headquarters K.16.d.9.6
Rgt HqP DEMICOURT 1/5000

Army Form C. 2118.

WAR DIARY
or
INTELLIGENCE SUMMARY.
(Erase heading not required.)

1st Company Machine Gun Corps

Instructions regarding War Diaries and Intelligence Summaries are contained in F. S. Regs., Part II. and the Staff Manual respectively. Title pages will be prepared in manuscript.

Place	Date	Hour	Summary of Events and Information	Remarks and references to Appendices
In the field	28/29		The following indirect fire was carried out during the night: Guns No 13, 14, 15 & 16 fired 7,000 rounds on enemy tracks and roads leading to GRAINCOURT.	
	29		(Gun No 6 Wright returned from leave to U.K. on this date)	
	29/30		Guns No 13, 14, 15 and 16 fired during the night on CAT TRENCH K.5.d. and on tracks in K.5.d. Number of rounds fired 8,600.	
	30/31		No firing took place during the night.	
	31/1.30		9,500 rounds were fired during the night on roads and tracks leading to GRAINCOURT. by the following guns. Nos 9, 10, 13, 14, 15 & 16.	

R.W.Weed. Captain
Commanding.
51 Machine Gun Company.

31st of Dec.

Herewith original copy of War
Diary for Feb. made up to 23rd ult.
as per instructions received from 17th
Batt. M.G.C. Headquarters.

R. Head
Capt
Commanding "B" Coy
1/3/18   17th Batt. M.G.C.

17th Bat. M.G.C. 51st Company

Army Form C. 2118.

WAR DIARY
or
INTELLIGENCE SUMMARY.
(Erase heading not required.)

Instructions regarding War Diaries and Intelligence Summaries are contained in F. S. Regs., Part II. and the Staff Manual respectively. Title pages will be prepared in manuscript.

Place	Date	Hour	Summary of Events and Information	Remarks and references to Appendices
In the field	1918 1/2 Jany.		Company in the line. H.Q. at K.15.d.9.11 reference DEMICOURT 1/10,000. During the night 13,000 rounds were fired by guns nos. 3,9,10,11,13,14,15,16 on roads leading to GRAINCOURT. 12,500 rounds were fired by 3,9,10,11,13,14,15 & 16 guns on lines, roads and dumps during the night.	
	2/3.		9,500 rounds were fired by 3,11,9,10,13,14,15 and 16 guns during the night on new work, roads and tracks. Several pack parties were dispersed.	
	3/4.		Gun No 8 was moved from K.10.d.1.5 to K.10.d.2.6. 10,000 rounds were fired by Nos. 3,11,13,14,15 and 16 guns on CAT TRENCH, new work and dumps, from K.c.c.2.4 also on roads on K.5.a.t.c.	
	4/5.		Party of enemy at K.5.d.0.7 were dispersed by sniping gun No 9. 9,000 rounds fired by S.O.S. Vorme guns on CAT TRENCH, roads and tracks. Stop any pioneer working parties on new work K.11. b.8.a. road K.5.cl. and K.11.b. and road K.6.c.7.K.12.a. Intermittent harassing fire was maintained on CAT TRENCH and buoy O.S.V.	
	5/6.		Total number of rounds fired 18,000.	
	6/7.		Company relieved at night by 32nd M.G. Coy and proceeded to SANDERS CAMP to the Ry. Main 57.e.	
	7/8.		During this tour in the line rations were taken up by limber as far as Coy HQtrs. Condition of roads good enough, shelled intermittently. No casualties were sustained by the transport. Weather most of	

As834. Wt. W4973/M687. 750,000. 8/16. D. D. & L. Ltd. Forms/C.2118/13.

WAR DIARY or INTELLIGENCE SUMMARY

Army Form C. 2118.

51st M.G. Coy.

Place	Date	Hour	Summary of Events and Information	Remarks and references to Appendices
Field	8/12		The time was very mild and almost thaw. An anti-metal relief took place half way through the tour. In camp Gun equipment cleaned, also overhauled. Men were bathed and anti gas equipment tested and inspected by Brigade Gas N.C.O. Capt R.J. Hay proceeded on leave to U.K. on 9th Feb. Lieut F.M. Nicholson assumed command. Company relieving 50th M.G. Cy on the line at night marching via BERTINCOURT and HERMIES. Company H.Qrs at K.4 & K.3 Ref map BOURSIES. Position 17 guns as before in this sector (see forwards) No firing was carried out. Relief completed by 8.30pm.	
	13			
	14/15		Well quiet S.O.S. sent up 10th rounds expending up 1 of the S.O.S. signal light from the fixture	
	15/16		5000 rounds were fired on observation and artillery on LK.4.B and squares E.28 d, K.4.a and K3b. 500 rounds were fired at 10/2m M.G. response to feet S.O.S. Enemy aeroplanes were driven off during the day by A.A. machine guns.	
	16/17		2 Lieut J.M. Lowther joins company as reinforcement	
	17/18		On co-operation with artillery harassing fire was carried out	

WAR DIARY
or
INTELLIGENCE SUMMARY.

51 M.G. Coy

Army Form C. 2118.

Date	Hour	Summary of Events and Information	Remarks and references to Appendices
18/19		During the night on trenches in N.2.b. Number of rounds fired 6,000. Additional emplacements were constructed at R.3 and R.3 positions during these days. L/Cpl Fleming accidentally wounded. Remained at duty.	
		7.C.17/7/17. 5,000 rounds were fired on roads and trenches in E.27 and Lock 6. R.3 a 8.6.	
19/20		In co-operation with the Artillery 5,000 rounds were fired on the same targets as night before.	
20/21"		2,500 rounds were fired on Spoilbank Trench, Saw Trench & Lock 6.	
21/22"		We fired 6,000 rounds on roads in N.3 & T.26 and N.4 c. In conjunction with the Artillery 5 guns fired on N.3 & S.8, N.3 a.76.	
22/23"		N.4 a r d — roads and trenches.	
		During the foregoing period work was carried on at all positions. Trenches improved and from Sea, Aircraft positions made with pit prop mountings.	

[signature] Captain
Commanding
51 Machine Gun Company.

WAR DIARY
INTELLIGENCE SUMMARY

7th ENTRENCHING BATTALION

Feb. 1918. REF. 57.C. FRANCE

Place	Date Feb	Hour	Summary of Events and Information	Remarks and references to Appendices
SALAMANCA / VITTORIA CAMP	24		Working party of 17 Officers + 900 O.R. working under R.E.'s in J34, digging + wiring new trench line.	
ditto	25		Working party as for 24th continuing trench.	
ditto	26		Same work carried out by 17 offr + 900 O.R. extending trench. Wiring commenced on 24th.	
ditto	27		Party of 18 Officers + 950 O.R. again provided. Battalion moved up to LONDON CAMP, between RUYAULCOURT + BERTINCOURT	
ditto	28		17 Officers + 900 O.R. provided for work as before. Draft of about 50 O.R. from 63rd Div. arrived, with Q.M. of HOWE Battalion	

Officer i/c
7th Entrenching
Battalion

E J Bennett Lt Col
Comd. No 7 Entrenching Battalion